Joaquim Nabuco, British Abolitionists and the End of Slavery in Brazil: Correspondence 1880–1905

Edited with an introduction by Leslie Bethell and José Murilo de Carvalho

INSTITUTE FOR THE STUDY OF THE
AMERICAS
UNIVERSITY OF LONDON · SCHOOL OF ADVANCED STUDY

British Library Cataloguing-in-Publication Data
A catalogue record for this book is available from the British Library

ISBN 978 1 900039 95 6

INSTITUTE FOR THE STUDY OF THE
AMERICAS
UNIVERSITY OF LONDON · SCHOOL OF ADVANCED STUDY

Institute for the Study of the Americas
University of London
Senate House
London WC1E 7HU

Telephone: 020 7862 8870
Fax: 020 7862 8886

Email: americas@sas.ac.uk
Web: www.americas.sas.ac.uk

CONTENTS

ACKNOWLEDGEMENTS

The editors wish to thank the University of Oxford Centre of Brazilian Studies for financial and logistical support and the Brazilian Academy of Letters for making it possible for José Murilo de Carvalho to spend two months in Oxford as Machado de Assis Visiting Professor of Brazilian Literature. The editors also thank Mario Helio at the Joaquim Nabuco Foundation in Recife for assistance in locating the letters from the British abolitionists to Joaquim Nabuco, Mathias Spektor for research assistance on Nabuco's correspondence in Rhodes House, Oxford, Sarah Rankin for secretarial assistance at the Oxford Centre for Brazilian Studies and James Dunkerley, then Director of the Institute for the Study of the Americas of the School of Advanced Study, University of London, for agreeing to publish an English edition of this book. A Brazilian edition was published by Topbooks, Rio de Janeiro, with the support of the Academia Brasileira de Letras. Thanks also to Karen Perkins of the Institute for the Study of the Americas and to Emily Morrell of the School of Advanced Study publications team for the production of this book.

Introduction

Leslie Bethell and José Murilo de Carvalho

A little studied aspect of the struggle to abolish slavery in Brazil in the 1880s is the relationship established and maintained between Joaquim Nabuco, the leading Brazilian abolitionist, and the British and Foreign Anti-Slavery Society in London. The correspondence between Nabuco and Charles Harris Allen, secretary of the Anti-Slavery Society, and other British abolitionists throughout the decade and beyond reveals a partnership consciously sought by Nabuco in order to internationalise the struggle. These letters provide a unique insight into the evolution of Nabuco's thinking on both slavery and abolition and at the same time a running commentary on the slow and (at least until 1887–8) uncertain progress of the abolitionist cause in Brazil.

Nabuco and abolition

The chapter on Massangana in Nabuco's autobiographical *Minha formação* is well known. In it he describes his visit in 1869, aged 20, to the chapel of the old sugar mill in Pernambuco which had been the property of his godmother D. Ana Rosa Falcão de Carvalho and where he had been raised. He entered the small enclosure that had been a cemetery for slaves. Standing among the crosses marking the graves, he looked back to his childhood and remembered the names of many of the captives that he had known. 'That was when I first had a perfectly clear idea of the moral problem of slavery and its mandatory solution,' he wrote. 'There and then, twenty years old, I resolved to devote my life, if it were given to me, to the service of the most generous of all the races' (that is to say, *a raça negra*). [Foi assim que o problema moral da escravidão se desenhou pela primeira vez aos meus olhos em sua nitidez perfeita e com a solução obrigatória . . . Então ali mesmo, aos vinte anos, formei a resolução devotar a minha vida, se assim me fosse dado, ao serviço da raça generosa entre todas]. *Minha formação* was, however, written 30 years after the episode described. The version it offers of the origin of Nabuco's decision to devote his life to the abolitionist movement in Brazil is thus a later construction. While there is no doubt that Nabuco was totally opposed to slavery throughout his life there is in fact no evidence, either in his extensive correspondence or in his diary, that the decision was taken earlier than 1879, the year he entered parliament for the first time.

Nabuco was eight years old when he left Massangana in 1857, following the death of his godmother. He was sent to Rio de Janeiro where he completed his secondary education at the Colégio de Pedro II. In 1866 he enrolled in the São Paulo law school. By then he had already come under the strong influence of his father, José Thomaz Nabuco de Araújo, senator and member of the council of state. Senator Nabuco was one of the few prominent politicians opposed to slavery at the time. As Minister of Justice (1853–7) he had been responsible for the repression of the last attempts to import slaves into Brazil after the Brazilian government, under severe British pressure, had in 1850–1 effectively abolished the transatlantic slave trade. And in the 1860s he was to play a leading role in drafting the first legislation aimed at the gradual abolition of slavery in Brazil.

Following the emancipation of the slaves in the United States during the Civil War (1861–5), Brazil and the Spanish colonies of Cuba and Puerto Rico were the only remaining slave societies in the Americas. There were one million and a half slaves in Brazil, 15 per cent of the population. Slavery was still to be found in every province, in the cities as well as the rural areas, in both non-export and export agriculture, but three provinces – Rio de Janeiro, Minas Gerais and São Paulo – now accounted for 70 per cent of the slave population and slaves were now more heavily concentrated in plantation agriculture, especially the coffee sector.

In April 1865 the emperor Dom Pedro II put the future of slavery in Brazil on the political agenda for the first time by inviting a well-known jurist Senator Pimenta Bueno, the future Visconde de São Vicente, to draft legislation to improve the condition of the slaves and to move towards gradual abolition. In January 1866 Pimenta Bueno submitted five draft bills for the consideration of the Conservative cabinet headed by the Marquês de Olinda. The most important proposed that in future children born to slave mothers would be free. Pimenta Bueno's proposals found little support. The main reason (or excuse) offered was Brazil's involvement since the end of 1864 in the War of the Triple Alliance (with Argentina and Uruguay) against Paraguay. Nevertheless, in August the Liberal-Progressive government of Zacarias de Góis e Vasconcelos caused a political commotion by stating in a reply to an appeal to the emperor from the Comité Français d'Emancipation, drafted with his full knowledge, that 'the emancipation of the slaves, a necessary consequence of the abolition of slave trade, is therefore only a question of form and opportunity'. The statement was repeated in the emperor's speech from the throne in May 1867. In the meantime, Pimenta Bueno's draft bills had been submitted to the council of state which was reluctant to act but which appointed Nabuco de Araújo chairman of a committee charged with consolidating them into a single bill. In July 1868, however, the emperor, anxious about the progress of the war against Paraguay, made a sudden and dramatic change of government, calling upon the Conservative Visconde de Itaboraí to replace Zacarias. Senator Nabuco headed the reaction to what he called a coup d'état. He helped found the radical newspaper *A Reforma* which adopted an anti-slavery stance, and later, in 1869, the Centro Liberal, which was the first political association in Brazil to include slave emancipation in its programme. But the Itaboraí cabinet was against all abolitionist projects and further discussion of *o elemento servil*, as it was called, was postponed for the next two years.

While his father was engaged with the issue of slavery in the senate and the council of state in Rio de Janeiro, Joaquim Nabuco was in São Paulo in the company of, among others, Castro Alves who was stirring up audiences with recitals of his abolitionist poetry. In 1869 he transferred to the law school in Recife where the atmosphere was less favourable to abolitionist ideas. Nevertheless, he wrote in 1870 a lengthy student text 'A escravidão', or rather the first two parts of a text: 'O crime' and 'A história do crime'. (The projected third part, 'A reparação do crime', was never written.)[1] His greatest success in Recife was his defence of a slave accused of murder and already condemned to death in a lower court. To assume such a defence in a region of powerful plantation owners, some of them his own kin, was without doubt a courageous act for a 20-year old law student. Nabuco's exceptional gifts as an orator were revealed for the first time, reinforced by his imposing physical presence. The defendant was saved from being hanged and sentenced instead to forced labour. In a letter to his father Nabuco admitted that his greatest wish was to see him president of the council of ministers for just two days so that he could abolish slavery by decree, thus becoming 'Brazil's Lincoln' (*o Lincoln brasileiro*).[2]

Nabuco graduated in November 1870 and returned to Rio de Janeiro where the following year he heard his father's speeches in the senate in defence of a bill introduced by the Conservative cabinet of the Visconde do Rio Branco to free children born of slave mothers. He wrote in *Minha Formação* that, at that time, he helped his father translate documents published in the *Anti-Slavery Reporter*, the journal of the British and Foreign Anti-Slavery Society. The law of free birth was finally approved on 28 September 1871 after the longest and most bitter series of debates in the history of the imperial parliament. By cutting off the internal supply of slaves, 20 years after the suppression of the transatlantic

1 'A escravidão' was not published at the time. The signed original, 230 handwritten pages, was donated to the Instituto Histórico e Geográfico Brasileiro by Nabuco's widow, Evelina, in September 1924: 'yet further proof' she wrote, 'of how slavery was his concern and abolition his ideal since almost childhood'. The text was published in the *Revista do Instituto Histórico e Geográfico Brasileiro* in 1949.

2 Carolina Nabuco, *The life of Joaquim Nabuco*, p. 18.

slave trade had cut off the external supply, the law condemned slavery in Brazil to *eventual* extinction. At the same time, there was to be a national register of slaves and a modest emancipation fund to stimulate the emancipation of slaves by slave-owners and the self-purchase of freedom by the slaves themselves. The 1871 law, however, posed no immediate threat to existing slave property. Moreover, the *ingênuos* (free born) were to remain with their masters until they were eight years old when they would be freed on payment of compensation or continue in semi-slavery until they reached 21 years. And the passage of the 1871 law, despite its extremely limited character, ended parliamentary debate on slavery for almost a decade – as many who finally and reluctantly voted for it intended.

In the years following his graduation, slavery was not Nabuco's central preoccupation. He was apparently uncertain about which road to take in life. He entered his father's law firm, but soon abandoned the legal profession. He dabbled with journalism and literature, writing for *A Reforma*, where he defended the Liberal cause, showing a particular interest in the separation of church and state. In 1872 he published his first book, on Camões and the Lusiads, and another in French, a dispute with Alexandre Dumas *fils* over the right of assassination. The same year he inherited Massangana, the decadent sugar mill which had belonged to his godmother. He sold it and decided to use the money to travel. He left Brazil in August 1873 and stayed in Europe until September the following year, mostly in Italy and France, where he published another book in French, *Amour et Dieu.* He spent a month (June 1874) in London without making contact with the British and Foreign Anti-Slavery Society.

On his return to Brazil Nabuco continued on an uncertain track until April 1876 when he began a diplomatic career. He was appointed attaché to the Brazilian legation in Washington, arriving there on 1 January 1877. It was not apparently hard work since he had time to finish another book in French, *l'Option*, about the French-German dispute over Alsace. He only remained in the Washington post for nine months. In October he was transferred to a similar post in the Brazilian legation in London, which he much preferred. However, this diplomatic post, too, was short-lived. In April 1878 he returned to Brazil following news of the death of his father, and remained there to contest a seat in parliament.

Before his death, Senator Nabuco de Araújo, with the support of the Barão de Vila Bela, the Liberal leader in the province, had prepared the ground for his son to be elected to parliament as a deputy for Pernambuco. Respect for his father's wishes, and the return of the Liberals to power in January 1878 after 10 years of Conservative rule, convinced Nabuco to enter politics, leaving behind his brief diplomatic career. In September the 29-year-old Nabuco had no problem in being elected to the Empire's seventeenth legislature, which was overwhelmingly Liberal, and took his seat in January 1879. His first speech was on the issue of religious freedom. It fell to Dr Jeronimo Sodré, a deputy from Bahia – physician, ultramontane Catholic, slave-owner but abolitionist, in a speech on 5 March to put slavery on the political agenda for the first time since 1871. Nabuco, however, soon adopted the issue of abolition as his own, even though the Liberal government led by the Visconde de Sinimbu supported slavery unconditionally. Nabuco's was to be the single most important voice, both inside and outside parliament, in favour of abolition until slavery was finally ended in Brazil in May 1888.

In *Minha formação* the driving force behind his decision to become actively involved in the struggle to abolish slavery is described as the 'dear blessed memory' of his childhood and of the suffering of the 'black saints', which was stimulated by the visit to the chapel at the Massangana sugar mill in 1869. It is no coincidence that he mentions that he had read *Uncle Tom's Cabin* a thousand times over. Nabuco comes close to apologising to the great English and North American abolitionists for making the almost scandalous confession of feeling a certain nostalgia for slavery. This reconstruction of the past a decade after abolition had been achieved offers a personal, moral, indeed sentimental explanation for his abolitionism. In his student text *A escravidão* written in 1870, a year after the visit to Massangana, in his book *O abolicionismo* published in London in 1883, and in the letters to the British abolitionists presented in this volume the reasons given for his commitment to the anti-slavery cause are somewhat different. Here slavery was challenged with the same arguments famously used by José Bonifacio de Andrada e Silva in his Representation to the Constituent Assembly of 1823, a year after Brazil's declaration of independence from Portugal: it was a crime, an outrage against civilisation, responsible for the country's backwardness, an obstacle to economic and political progress and to the construction of a nation.

The initiative that brought Nabuco international renown as the champion of the slaves in Brazil and first brought him in contact with the British and Foreign Anti-Slavery Society was a speech in parliament on 30 September 1879 denouncing the British-owned St John Del Rey Mining Company. The company kept slaves in captivity in its Morro Velho gold mine that it had bought from the Cata Branca and Cocais mining companies in 1845, with a contractual clause to free them after 14 years' service. Twenty years had, however, gone by, as Nabuco pointed out, without any steps being taken to secure their freedom. Nabuco's speech had repercussions in France, with comment in the *Revue des deux Mondes*, and more particularly in Great Britain. The secretary of the Anti-Slavery Society, Charles H. Allen, sent him a letter from London dated 8 January 1880, congratulating him for his defence of the Morro Velho slaves (letter I: 1). And through Charles Williams, director of Cocais mines, he forwarded a resolution in similar terms from the society's committee (letter I: 2).[3] Nabuco replied to Allen at length on 8 April 1880 (I: 3), thanking the Anti-Slavery Society for its gesture of support, explaining the nature of the abolitionist struggle in Brazil and affirming his commitment to the cause in which he was now fully engaged. '[. . .] I assure', he wrote, 'you will always find me at the fighting post I now occupy [. . .] I place the emancipation interest beyond any other [. . .] Compared to this great social reform [. . .] political reforms remain in the shade'. Allen's letter of 8 January and Nabuco's reply of 8 April mark the beginning of a long and fruitful relationship between Nabuco and British abolitionists.

In his letter of 8 April Nabuco told Allen that he was planning to submit to parliament a bill for the total abolition of slavery in Brazil on 1 January 1890. He did not expect it to pass in view of the existing strength of pro-slavery opinion, in the Liberal as well as the Conservative party. But he planned to introduce it in every session until as a result of the 'spread of moral conviction' and increasing pressure from abolitionist opinion it was eventually passed, predicting that 'the frontier of the next decade shall not be crossed in Brazil . . . by any man calling himself a slave'. The proposal he did indeed put before parliament in August was moderate, inasmuch as it not only envisaged a 10-year period before the total emancipation of the slaves but offered compensation to the slave-owners, as Britain had done in its colonies half a century earlier. Nevertheless, the bill failed to make progress. Initially, 38 deputies signed a motion for an early decision on whether to hold a debate on the bill, but after the Liberal president of the council of ministers, Senator José Antônio Saraiva, made it a question of confidence in his government only 18 deputies (14 of them from the North, including seven from Pernambuco) actually voted for a debate and the bill was quietly withdrawn.

On 7 September 1880, Nabuco together with other colleagues meeting in his home in Rio de Janeiro (Rua Bela da Princesa, now called Correia Dutra) founded the Sociedade Brasileira contra Escravidão. He himself was elected president and the engineer André Rebouças treasurer. The sociedade was certainly inspired by the Anti-Slavery Society in London and its creation facilitated easier and closer contacts between abolitionists in the two countries. An official letter from the sociedade dated 8 October 1880, informing its British counterpart of its foundation and enclosing a copy of its manifesto, expressed the hope that the two societies would be able to work in close cooperation (I: 5). Allen immediately answered with a promise of full collaboration (I: 6).

In December, taking advantage of the parliamentary recess, Nabuco left for

3 The correspondence between Nabuco and the English abolitionists was divided into three groups: I 1880 to 1889; II 1899 to 1902; III Epilogue 1904–5.

Europe in order to raise international awareness of the anti-slavery movement in Brazil. In Lisbon he was received in the chamber of deputies as the champion of the abolitionist struggle in the Brazilian legislature. In Madrid he was honoured by the Sociedad Abolicionista Española. His main objective, however, was to establish direct personal contact with the British and Foreign Anti-Slavery Society in London which he and his abolitionist colleagues regarded as 'the first and most influential organisation of its kind in the world' and whose cooperation was therefore essential in the fight against slavery in Brazil (I: 7).

Britain and abolition

By the 1880s Britain could claim to have been engaged in the struggle to abolish the slave trade and slavery, national and international, for the best part of a century.

In 1783 London Quakers, in response to an appeal from their brethren in Philadelphia, had created the first abolitionist organisation in Britain, the Committee on the Slave Traffic. Four years later, in 1787, the Committee for the Abolition of the Slave Trade was formed, most of whose members again were Quakers. And after a campaign led by William Wilberforce, Thomas Clarkson and others lasting 20 years, the British parliament in 1807 abolished the slave trade to Britain's colonies.

Britain now dedicated itself to persuading, bribing and, if necessary, forcing other nations involved in the slave trade to follow its example: first, by declaring the slave trade illegal, and then by making the ban effective, not least by permitting the Royal Navy to play a leading role in its suppression. For example, anti-slave trade treaties were signed with Portugal in 1810, 1815 and 1817 and, after it had secured its independence from Portugal, with Brazil in 1826. It was in fulfilment of its treaty obligations with Britain that Brazil in 1831 introduced legislation making the importation of slaves illegal.

The British slave trade had ended but slavery continued in the British colonies. In 1823, the abolitionists, again with Wilberforce in the forefront and a strong Quaker presence, founded the Society for the Mitigation and Gradual Abolition of Slavery throughout the British Dominions (also known as the Anti-Slavery Society) whose purpose was to improve the condition of slaves and to promote the gradual abolition of slavery. When Wilberforce retired from parliament in 1825, Henry Brougham and more especially Thomas Fowell Buxton took over the leadership of the society. Dissatisfied with the results of the parliamentary struggle, a more radical group headed by the Quaker Joseph Sturge decided to create an Agency committee in 1831 to pursue immediate and unconditional abolition. The committee ran a widespread public campaign. More than 1,300 local committees were created, 5,500 petitions sent to parliament. Finally, in 1833 the British parliament abolished slavery throughout the British empire (from August 1834), providing for the payment of £20m to the slave-owners and establishing a period of 'apprenticeship' in which freed slaves, except for children under six years old, were obliged to work for their masters until August 1840. After protests from Sturge and the Agency committee about the poor treatment of the 'apprentices', the six-year apprenticeship was reduced to four years and in August 1838 around 800,000 slaves were finally freed.

Sturge did not rest after this victory. Slavery continued outside the British empire – in the United States, in Brazil, and in Cuba and Puerto Rico. Moreover, the transatlantic slave trade to Brazil and Cuba, albeit illegal, continued on a much higher scale than 30 years earlier. Sturge, as a pacifist, was opposed to philanthropic interventions using force. He believed that the slave trade would only come to an end when slavery itself was abolished throughout the Americas by means of moral and religious persuasion. Determined to internationalise the struggle against slavery, he founded on 17 April 1839 the British and Foreign Anti-Slavery Society, with the support of Quakers, Baptists, Methodists and other non-conformist churches. To mark its international character the new society organised the first World Anti-Slavery Convention in the Freemason's Hall, London on 12 June 1840, attended by abolitionists from various countries, especially the United States and France. That same year, the new society sent a secret delegation to Brazil to study the local situation. Unfortunately, no information about the outcome, if any, of this visit has been found.

Thomas Fowell Buxton, the recognised successor of Wilberforce – who had died in 1833 – as leader of the abolitionist cause in parliament (although he lost his seat in 1837), was a member of the committee of the British and Foreign Anti-Slavery Society. But in his book *The Slave Trade and its Remedy*, written in 1838 and published in two parts in 1839 and 1840, he advocated a different approach to the problem of the slave trade and slavery. In June 1839, two months after the creation of the Anti-Slavery Society, he set up the society for the Extinction of the Slave Trade and for the Civilization of Africa, with Prince Albert as its president. The foreign slave trade, he argued, could indeed be extinguished before slavery itself was abolished. Unlike Sturge, he did not oppose diplomatic pressure and the use of force by Britain, but in his view the Navy could be more effective if it were to concentrate its efforts on the African coast. This would, however, not be sufficient. Nothing less than the economic, moral and social regeneration of Africa through agriculture, commerce and Christianity, and destruction of the slave trade at its source through legitimate trade with Africa, would be required. After the failure of the Niger expedition in 1841 and various African colonisation schemes, the Society was wound up in January 1843, leaving the field clear for the British and Foreign Anti-Slavery Society. Buxton retired, and died two years later.

The Anti-Slavery Society maintained its commitment to the suppression of transatlantic slave trade, but remained opposed to Britain's self-appointed role as the world's anti-slave trade policeman. It preferred to concentrate on abolishing slavery – and, as a consequence, the slave trade – by bringing moral pressure to bear on the United States, Brazil and Spain. When the slave trade reached new heights in the late 1840s despite the efforts of the Navy, the Anti-Slavery Society, backed by manufacturing and commercial interests, seemed to be winning the argument. Not only the morality but also the efficacy of Britain's anti-slave trade policy was increasingly questioned, and there was a real possibility that it would be finally dismantled as a costly failure. The British Foreign Secretary, Lord Palmerston, however, always contemptuous of the society's pacifism and convinced that the slave trade could be crushed and slavery delivered a severe blow by cutting off the external supply of slaves once the British naval force was fully operational, had the last word. In 1850, the South American squadron was reinforced and given orders to capture slave ships in Brazilian territorial waters. In the face of a serious threat to Brazil's sovereignty, political stability and economic prosperity, the Brazilian government – the first since 1831, it should be said, capable of doing so – finally took steps effectively to end the slave trade. Brazil could no longer resist the 'pressure of ideas of the times in which we live', declared Paulino José Soares de Souza, Brazilian Foreign Minister, by which he meant the pressure of the British government and the Royal Navy.

Official British pressure on Brazil in relation to slavery weakened considerably after the abolition of the slave trade. But the British government continued to demand the freedom of the so-called *emancipados*, the slaves found on ships earlier captured by British warships and liberated by the Anglo-Brazilian mixed court in Rio de Janeiro. The Anti-Slavery Society, however, sought to maintain the international moral pressure on Brazil. Along with the Comité Français d'Emancipation and the Sociedad Abolicionista Española it sponsored an international Anti-Slavery Convention in Paris in 1867. And Louis Alexis Chamerovzow, secretary of the society (1851–70), and Joseph Cooper, a future honorary secretary, were two of the signatories to an appeal made to the Brazilian people in 1869 by the newly-formed International Abolitionist Association based in Paris, reinforcing the appeal to the emperor by the French Comité in 1866, to put an end to slavery, 'the disgrace of humanity'. Brazil ran the risk, warned the Association, of becoming 'the last Christian nation to maintain slavery'.[4] The Anti-Slavery Society was certainly aware of the abolitionist efforts of Senator Nabuco de Araújo. In July 1869, it published in its journal, the *Anti-Slavery Reporter*, an open letter from the senator to the Constitutional Democratic Society of Limeira, São Paulo on the question.[5]

4 The letter was published in *O Abolicionista* on 1 December 1880, p. 3.

5 The letter from Senator Nabuco is dated 26 April 1869. See *Um Estadista do Império*, pp.

But there is no evidence of any direct contact between the society and Brazilian abolitionists until the letter from its secretary, Charles Allen, to Nabuco on 8 January 1880, Nabuco's reply of 8 April and the formal exchange of letters on the establishment of the Brazilian Anti-Slavery Society in September–October – and no personal contact until Nabuco's arrival in London in February 1881.

Nabuco in London, 1881–4

There are two chapters on London in *Minha formação* (and another two about British influence on the author). Although Nabuco's education, like that of all his generation, had had a stronger focus on France, and French was for him almost a second language, his heart seemed to be more inclined to Britain and London. 'The strongest impression made on me was not Paris but London,' he wrote. 'London for me was what Rome would have been if I had lived in the 2nd to 4th centuries.' London was the centre of global economic and political power, the imperial metropolis, majestic, calm, sure of itself. He was impressed by the parks, the architecture, the streets, the squares and, not least, the Thames. There was no doubt more artistic exuberance in Paris but, he concluded, 'the fact is that I loved London more than any other thing and place I know . . . I return from England . . . fascinated by London, touched by the beginnings of Anglomania'.

The title of the second chapter on London is an address: 32 Grosvenor Gardens. This was the home of the Brazilian minister, Francisco Inácio de Carvalho Moreira, one of the most distinguished diplomats of the empire, who had been given the title of Barão de Penedo in 1864. Penedo was the son of a plantation owner from Alagoas. He had studied at Brazil's two leading law schools, Recife and São Paulo. After a brief period in politics, on the part of the Conservative party, he was appointed minister plenipotentiary to the United States in 1851. In 1855 he was transferred to London. With a few interruptions, the longest between 1863 and 1866 caused by the break in diplomatic relations between Brazil and England as a result of the so-called 'Christie affair', he stayed in London as Brazilian minister until 1888, under both Conservative or Liberal cabinets.[6]

In the nineteenth century, London was by far the most important of Brazil's legations abroad. The Brazilian minister in London was responsible for all Brazil's external payments and also negotiated Brazilian loans with N.M. Rothschild & Sons, from 1855 the semi-official bankers of the empire. Penedo negotiated six such loans. It was customary at the time to pay commission, generally 2 per cent, to loan negotiators. When the commission was not included in the contract, they would receive informal 'gifts'. Penedo once admitted that

670–1.

6 On Penedo, see Renato de Mendonça, *Um diplomata na corte da Inglaterra.*

£200,000 had passed through his hands from the Rothschilds. It was from this source, and from his own financial investments, often on the advice of the Rothschilds, that Penedo was able to cover the expenses of the legation – the rent on the building alone cost £1,400 a year, half Penedo's annual salary of £2,800 at that time – and maintain his high standard of living.

Number 32 Grosvenor Gardens, still standing today, to which the legation moved in 1873, was a meeting point for London's high society, including the Prince of Wales, the future king Edward VII, members of the aristocracy – and the Rothschilds. In this mansion Penedo would regularly host banquets for more than 60 guests prepared by the legation's famous chef Cortais, a former employee of the grand duke of Russia. Penedo offered such a banquet for D. Pedro II on his second visit to London in 1876. The thrifty emperor did not fail to comment on his minister's luxurious lifestyle, forcing Penedo to explain the origin of his funds.

At 32 Grosvenor Gardens, Nabuco found a warm welcome when he visited London as a tourist in June 1874, as an attaché to the legation from October 1877 to April 1878, and as a deputy, ex-deputy and propagandist for abolition during the 1880s. Penedo treated him with almost parental care: he had after all been a colleague of Nabuco's father at the Recife law school and Nabuco himself had been a colleague of one of Penedo's sons, Artur, at the São Paulo law school. Nabuco was provided with accommodation and frequent invitations to dinner (where he was particularly appreciative of the food prepared by Cortais). He wrote in *Minha formação*: 'What prevented me from being Republican in my youth was most likely my being aware of, and impressed by, the aristocratic way of life.'

On his third visit to London in February 1881, without refusing Penedo's hospitality – he was once again a guest at 32 Grosvenor Gardens – nor failing to appreciate the city's charms, Nabuco put all his energy into the campaign in which he was now engaged. He immediately sought out the British and Foreign Anti-Slavery Society, which welcomed him with every honour. On 4 March it held a session officially to introduce Nabuco, on which occasion he spoke as usual at some length. On 23 March, he was offered a splendid breakfast in the Charing Cross Hotel presided over by Thomas Fowell Buxton, son of the famous abolitionist of the same name who was about to become president of the society. One hundred and fifty people were present, including the outgoing president Samuel Gurney, the secretary Charles Allen, the treasurer Joseph Allen, and 11 members of the House of Commons. There was a brief speech by Buxton and another 'rather long' speech (according to *The Times*) by Nabuco. The banquet was widely covered by the London press – and by the Rio de Janeiro press. The *Jornal do Comércio* published an article from its London correspondent. The 'British connection' had become a reality. From that point Nabuco's relations with the Anti-Slavery Society, especially with its secretary Charles Allen, became ever closer. As early as March 1881, Nabuco told Allen that he had found in him more than just a supporter of the cause but a close friend (I: 15). A sincere friendship can be deduced from the terms of the correspondence between the two, which endured until Allen's death in December 1904.

Nabuco stayed in London until the end of the Brazilian legislative recess in April 1881. When the chamber of deputies was dissolved on 30 June he offered himself as a candidate for the first district of the 'corte' (the capital, Rio de Janeiro) in the elections to be held on 31 October. But despite the strong campaign in his favour run by the abolitionists, he was defeated and forced to leave parliament. (I: 17 and 19). In his frustration, and despite being accused by some of too readily abandoning the struggle for abolition, he left Brazil in December and returned to his beloved London, as he put it 'in virtually enforced exile'. He wrote to Allen that he had decided to spend two years or so in London (letter I: 19). Allen immediately replied inviting him to the monthly committee meeting of the Anti-Slavery Society, which he had in any case a right to attend as a corresponding member (I: 21 and 22).

During his stay in London, this time for almost two and a half years, from December 1881 to April 1884, Nabuco resided at three addresses: 19 Brook Street (until July 1883), 20A Maddox Street (until March 1884) and 33 Davies Street. He earned his living as correspondent of the *Jornal do Comércio* (arranged for him by Penedo, a friend of one of the owners, Francisco Antônio Picot) and as a consultant to English firms with investments in Brazil (many of them also put his way by Penedo). In July 1882 he petitioned the Brazilian parliament demanding this time not as in August 1880 abolition after 10 years but the 'total emancipation of the slaves, either immediately or within a short term, which however must be now defined' (I: 30 and 33). He petitioned the Institute of International Law meeting in Turin in September 1882 and attended the International Law Association meeting in Milan in September 1883, both with support from the Anti-Slavery Society. He attended countless abolitionist meetings but spent a good part of his time in the British Museum gathering material for his book *O Abolicionismo*, which was published in London in August 1883. He also made extensive use of *The Times* to promote the cause of abolition in Brazil.

The Nabuco strategy

Since 1879, when Nabuco's speech in parliament on the question of the slaves held by the St John del Rey Mining Company echoed around Europe and caused an immediate reaction from the British and Foreign Anti-Slavery Society, Nabuco and other Brazilian abolitionists had become increasingly aware of the importance of mobilising international public opinion in support of their movement. In Brazil itself, public opinion had not yet been mobilised on the question and there was no sign of any weakening in the resistance to abolition in parliament. But the Brazilian elite, including the emperor, could be influenced by international, especially British and French, opinion. Persistent British pressure for the liberation of the *emancipados*, the appeal of the French Comité d'Emancipation to the emperor in 1866 and the message to the Brazilian people from the International Abolitionist Association in 1869, had all undoubtedly contributed to the introduction and passage of the law of free birth in 1871.

One of the first measures taken by the Sociedade Brasileira contra Escravidão in 1880, as we have seen, was to announce its existence to its peer associations abroad and to distribute copies of its manifesto in English and French. The choice of the British and Foreign Anti-Slavery Society as the Brazilian society's principal interlocutor was logical. The British society was by far the world's most influential abolitionist society. Once Nabuco had established himself in London the society helped him set up an efficient propaganda scheme for the Brazilian abolitionist movement. Nabuco would give information to Allen who would be responsible for releasing it to the press, especially the influential *Times*. And when he was unable to do so, which rarely happened, Allen would publish it in the society's own journal, the *Anti-Slavery Reporter*. *The Times* was the ideal medium because of its influence in and outside Great Britain. Nabuco himself wrote in one of his letters to Allen that in Brazil, '*The Times* seems the voice of civilisation [a voz da civilização]' (I: 45). In a letter to the newspaper's editor, Allen commented that publicity in *The Times* was a major asset to the Brazilian abolitionists, 'the [Brazilian] planters being peculiarly sensitive to the criticism of the English people' (I: 57). *The Times* took a clear abolitionist stance and seldom refused to publish letters from Allen and news stories sent by Allen from Nabuco's letters. When the newspaper published some unfavourable article, Nabuco would be anxious and insist on replying. It is highly unlikely that the Brazilian planters in general were in fact so sensitive to criticism from *The Times*, but the Brazilian political elite, imbued with Western values and concerned with Brazil's external image, certain were.

Information on British support for abolition in Brazil reached the Brazilian government and the Brazilian parliament through another channel. The Brazilian minister Penedo forwarded to Itamaraty (the Brazilian Foreign Ministry) in Rio de Janeiro articles published in *The Times* and other newspapers about Brazilian slavery and about Nabuco's activities in promoting its abolition. Penedo did not share Nabuco's enthusiasm for the anti-slavery cause, but he did not seem to have objected to his friend's campaign, even during the pro-slavery Conservative government of Cotegipe (August 1885–March 1888).

There is no sign of any dissension between them. Nor did Penedo ever ask Nabuco to moderate his position.

The Brazilian press was also part of the propaganda machine. The journal of the Sociedade Brasileira contra Escravidão, *O Abolicionista*, lasted only 13 months and had only a small circulation. But *A Gazeta de Notícias*, in whose columns the radical abolitionist José do Patrocínio first came to prominence, the weekly *Revista Ilustrada* with its brilliant caricatures by the Italian-Brazilian artist Ângelo Agostini, more particularly *A Gazeta da Tarde* and later (from September 1887) *Cidade do Rio*, all played an important part in the struggle for abolition. Nabuco's own efforts in 1882 (and again in 1885) to found a daily newspaper failed for lack of funds. But he had good contacts in the most influential newspaper in the capital, the *Jornal do Comércio*. In addition to articles by its own correspondent in London (Nabuco), the *Jornal* would often reproduce articles from *The Times* and other European newspapers. Although it did not ostensibly take sides, one of its editors, Gusmão Lobo, was a committed abolitionist and a friend of Nabuco, and the editor-in-chief, Luis de Castro, also discreetly supported the cause. Nabuco later wrote for, and was correspondent in London for, the Republican newspaper *O Paiz*, founded by Quintino Bocaiúva in 1884, who considered abolitionist propaganda useful in his criticism of the political system of the empire. Another important newspaper in the Brazilian capital was the *Rio News*, owned by an American, Andrew Jackson Lamoureux, who translated into English the documents provided by the Sociedade Brasileira contra Escravidão and later the Confederação Abolicionista and disseminated them to the influential English-speaking community of Rio de Janeiro.

The Nabuco-Allen partnership worked efficiently towards its objective of giving an international dimension to the Brazilian anti-slavery movement, thus increasing the pressure on the emperor, the Brazilian government, the representatives of the Brazilian slave-owners in parliament and the Brazilian elite more generally. The strategy, however, was not without risk for Nabuco. During his journey to Europe in 1881 he was accused by the supporters of slavery of sullying the name of Brazil abroad by disclosing the evils of slavery and therefore of lacking patriotism. This accusation upset him considerably and he defended himself against it on several occasions. A good part of his speech at the breakfast in his honour offered by the British Anti-Slavery Society in London in March 1881 was devoted to the topic. He was accused, he said, of encouraging 'a kind of European moral intervention in our domestic affairs and of displaying to the world a national misfortune that should be jealously hidden from view'. His answer was that he was 'only too glad when liberal opinion of any party abroad applauds our work ... We are not willing to build ... a Chinese wall to protect slaveholders from the general influences which have made the world incompatible with slavery' (I: 14 note).[7]

7 See *O Abolicionista* dated 01/05/1881, pp. 5–6.

An even more emphatic rejection of the accusation of unpatriotic behaviour was provoked by an article by Professor Goldwin Smith published in *Macmillan's Magazine* in 1886, in which the author criticised the fact that W.L. Garrison, the North American abolitionist, had sought the support of English public opinion for his movement. Nabuco wrote a detailed rebuttal in defence of Garrison, but also in his own defence, and asked Allen if he could get it published in the *Times*.[8] He argued that an action that tried to raise Brazil to the level of civilisation already achieved by other nations could not be considered unpatriotic. No greater service could be rendered to Brazil than for the entire world to condemn slavery, since his country's redemption would be achieved much earlier than through his own voice alone (I: 65 note). Nabuco's reply to Goldwin Smith recalls a passage in *O abolicionismo* in which Nabuco denounces what he calls 'the corruption of patriotism [*a corrupção do patriotismo*]', the use of patriotism to defend an institution condemned by the entire civilised world. Fundamentally, Nabuco believed the abolition of slavery was a question of civilisation, of the moral progress of humankind, of the spread of universal values which in the end no country could escape. True patriotism, he argued, meant that the country must belong to the civilised world. And when Nabuco argued that the end of slavery was an indispensable condition for building a nation, he was of course working with a different concept of the national interest from that of the slave-owners and their representatives, much closer to that of José Bonifácio at the time of Brazil's independence.

Nabuco in Brazil, 1884–7

After almost two and a half years in London Nabuco returned to Brazil in May 1884. He planned to be away for some four months. He was in poor health; he had been working too hard and needed a holiday; he was suffering from homesickness and 'want of my native sun'. But his decision may have also been influenced by the fact that the abolitionist movement outside parliament had gained considerable momentum during his absence. In August 1883 a number of abolitionist societies had come together to form Confederação Abolicionista committed to immediate abolition without indemnification. In March 1884, a month before his decision to return, Ceará had become the first of Brazil's provinces to abolish slavery (to be followed in July by Amazonas). Perhaps, Nabuco told Allen, 'some energetic kind of action' was required of him (I: 49).

On 6 June 1884 Senator Manuel Pinto de Sousa Dantas was invited by Dom Pedro II to form a government, the sixth Liberal government in six years, and the first with an anti-slavery agenda. The most important of the various bills

8 This was one of the few cases when Allen did not succeed in including a letter from Nabuco in *The Times*. It was later published in the *Anti-Slavery Reporter*.

he introduced was the one to free slaves over 60 years of age. It represented the first direct challenge to existing slave property in Brazil. It was also somewhat more far-reaching than first appeared since many slaves under 60 had been registered as older than they in fact were so that their owners could claim they had been legally imported before the 1831 law prohibiting the importation of slaves into Brazil. Moreover, no compensation would be offered to the owners of these slaves on the grounds that slaves were not property and slavery had no moral or legal legitimacy. The movement for the liberation of slaves aged 60 and over without indemnification gained extraordinary force in the following weeks, especially in the press, where abolitionists defending Dantas adopted the names of distinguished British and North American abolitionists. Nabuco, for example, was Garrison, Rui Barbosa both Lord Grey and Lincoln, Gusmão Lobo Clarkson, and so on. But Dantas could not in the end unify the Liberal party behind his bill; too many Liberal deputies were hostile or indifferent. At the end of July he was defeated on a motion of confidence by 59 votes to 52 in the chamber and the bill had to be dropped. The emperor, however, against the wishes of a majority of the council of state, granted Dantas the dissolution of parliament. And Nabuco immediately became a candidate for the first district of Pernambuco (the city of Recife).

The elections of December 1884, in which the key issue, indeed virtually the only issue, was the Dantas bill, were the first to be held under the new rules introduced by the Saraiva law of 1881. Elections were now direct and the vote was restricted to literates. The abolitionists expected to be the main beneficiaries of these changes since they were expected to reduce fraud and increase the weight of the urban vote. It was, Nabuco wrote to Allen, 'the first election of its kind in Brazil, quite an English or American election, disputed in public meetings, instead of the corrupt system of intimidating and buying votes in which slavery puts its force. The public mind is very excited' (I: 54). He was nevertheless defeated in Recife, though only narrowly, and because of some disturbances and accusations of irregularities the result was declared invalid. In a second election in January 1885 the Conservative candidate Machado Portela chose to abstain and Nabuco therefore won unopposed, only for the chamber when it met in May to overturn the result and award the seat to Machado Portela. However, on the death of the representative of the fifth district of Pernambuco the other Liberal candidates stood aside in favour of Nabuco, and on 5 June he was duly re-elected to the chamber (I: 51, 54 and 55). Allen was informed of everything and saw to it that both the bad and the good news were inserted in *The Times*. That newspaper's endorsement, he repeated in a letter on 22 June, was the most powerful indication of the support of English public opinion for the cause of Brazilian abolition (I: 57).

Before Nabuco finally re-entered parliament, after an absence of four years, Dantas had been defeated again in the newly elected chamber in which the Liberals had an even bigger majority – by 52 votes to 50. He failed to persuade the emperor to grant him a second dissolution and was forced to resign, being replaced by Saraiva, who on 13 August secured the chamber's approval of a much milder version of Dantas's bill: slaves aged 60 and over would be freed but forced to work for three more years, at which point the slave-owners would receive compensation for their emancipation; masters who emancipated slaves under 60 would be indemnified from an enhanced emancipation fund (at levels above the market price for slaves), and in these cases freed slaves were obliged to provide their services for a further five years. Shortly before the bill was approved, Nabuco wrote a long emotional letter to Allen, vehemently condemning what he called a 'shameful act through which slavery will be perpetuated in the National Debt'. The chamber of deputies, he said, had become a 'Moroccos slave market'. The bill, he continued, liquidated slavery [sic] 'on the best possible terms for the persons interested in it'. And he ended by accusing the Saraiva cabinet of seeking to 'make the death of slavery and its burying so soft that no one be aware of it – neither the master nor the slave, the country nor the world' (I: 59). Even so, Conservative opposition was such that Saraiva did not feel he had enough support to have his bill approved in the senate. He therefore resigned, and the emperor called upon Senator João Maurício Wanderley, Barão de Cotegipe, leader of the Conservative party, to perform the task. The bill was passed in the senate in August and became the Saraiva-Cotegipe law, better known as the Sexagenarian law, on 28 September 1885, the 14th anniversary of the Law of the Free Womb.

The Liberal chamber had in the meantime passed a motion of no confidence in Cotegipe, and on 26 October he called for new elections. In the elections on 15 January 1886 Nabuco was again candidate for Recife (I: 63). And he was once again defeated in what proved to be a Conservative landslide. Disenchanted and disillusioned, Nabuco spent much of the following year writing for the Rio press and publishing pamphlets, including *O erro do Imperador* and *O eclipse do abolicionismo* in which he bitterly criticised the emperor for having first encouraged the abolitionists with the choice of Dantas and then surrendered the government to the uncompromisingly pro-slavery Cotegipe. He was already thinking of returning to London to earn his living but acknowledged that his absence again would be detrimental to the Liberal and, more important, the abolitionist cause. He felt frustrated by having to solve at the same time his own financial problems and his country's principal social problem (I: 65).

Nabuco did eventually return to London in April 1887 – this time as correspondent for *O Paiz*. In addition to the meetings of the Anti-Slavery Society, he was honoured to accept an invitation to a reception at the home of the former British Prime Minister William Gladstone, thanks to the mediation of Allen, who accompanied him (I: 71). It was an informal endorsement by the British Liberal establishment of his campaign. For all his kindnesses since their first meeting in February 1881 Nabuco thanked Allen by presenting him with a Brazilian parrot as a gift. Allen mentions in more than one letter how fond he had become of the bird (I: 74 and 79). But it apparently never adapted to the English climate and never spoke.

Nabuco did not stay long in London on this occasion. With the appointment of Machado Portela to a ministerial post, there had to be under the rules of that time a new election in Recife. Nabuco returned from London in August 1887 and contested the election on 14 September, defeating the minister by 1,407 to 1,270 votes in another memorable campaign. He sent an enthusiastic letter to Allen on 16 September, describing his 'tremendous victory', a 'grand new event in our history!' (I: 73). Allen had the letter published in *The Times* and sent a copy to Gladstone (I: 74), who expressed his 'most cordial satisfaction' at the news of Nabuco's return to parliament (I: 75).

Abolition

Following the passage of the Sexagenarian law in September 1885 no further measures towards the liberation of Brazil's remaining three-quarters of a million to one million slaves were expected from the Cotegipe government – and none was forthcoming. Meanwhile, and partly as a consequence, the abolitionist movement outside parliament grew steadily in strength and became increasingly vociferous – and radical. At the same time, the slave system's natural decline accelerated as a result of two new factors: first, the mass desertion by slaves on the coffee plantations of São Paulo and elsewhere, aided by the abolitionists, and facilitated by the refusal of many positivist, abolitionist and republican junior army officers either to maintain order in the countryside or to pursue and capture fugitive slaves; secondly, an increase in the voluntary liberation of slaves in return for promises to remain on the plantations by owners fearful of the total disintegration of plantation labour. Equally significant in the demise of slavery in Brazil was the fact that the coffee *fazendeiros* of São Paulo, where the demand for slave labour was greatest, believed they had found an alternative source of labour: European, mainly Italian, immigrants. São Paulo received around 6,000 European immigrant workers each year between 1882 and 1886; 32,000 in 1887; over 90,000 in 1888.

In June 1887 the ailing emperor had gone to Europe for medical treatment leaving as regent his daughter Princess Isabel, who was known to be sympathetic to the cause of abolition. In November Nabuco travelled once more to Europe, this time with the objective of persuading Pope Leo XIII to issue a bull condemning slavery. Nabuco calculated that if the Pope were to speak out Isabel, who was also well known for the strength of her religious sentiments, would take the necessary steps to end what remained of the slave system in Brazil. In London Nabuco's friends in the Anti-Slavery Society, many of them Quakers, obtained a letter of introduction to the Pope from Cardinal Manning, Archbishop of Westminster and head of the Catholic Church in Great Britain (I: 76 and 77). After waiting around in Rome for a month, on 10 February Nabuco was finally received by the Pope who promised a papal encyclical condemning slavery. In the event Cotegipe managed to have its publication postponed, but Nabuco's account of his meeting with the Pope was published in *O Paiz* and became generally known.

The Conservative government and the Conservative party were by now deeply divided on the question of abolition. The slave system was clearly breaking down, its final demise accompanied by a rising level of violence; and there were exaggerated fears of a major social upheaval. In March 1888 Cotegipe was persuaded to resign and another Conservative leader, João Alfredo Correia de Oliveira, who had indicated his willingness to form a government committed to the immediate and unconditional abolition of slavery and the emancipation of Brazil's remaining 250–500,000 slaves, took office. Nabuco, who was in London at the time, immediately began his return journey to Brazil. On 30 March he reached Recife and on 18 April he was in Rio de Janeiro ready to lead the final battle for the approval of an abolition bill by parliament. On 8 May a bill for the abolition of slavery without compensation was submitted to parliament. Nabuco took it upon himself to ensure that the bill passed rapidly through the chamber as a matter of urgency, in particular by ensuring that the Liberals supported the bill, albeit introduced by a Conservative government. Since to a large extent it represented the legal recognition of a fait accompli, the voting process was almost perfunctory. The bill was approved by 83 votes to nine on its second reading on 9 May. It was given a third reading and sent to the senate the following day. Dantas took responsibility for the bill when it was submitted to the senate on 11 May. It was approved on its second reading the following day, with only six votes against (including that of Cotegipe). On 13 May, after a third and final reading in the senate, the Princess Regent signed the so-called Lei Áurea (Golden law) in the Paço da Cidade in Rio de Janeiro, from whose windows Nabuco addressed the large crowd gathered outside. Perhaps the single most important law in the history of Brazil was also the shortest. It consisted of two articles only:

Art. 1. Slavery in Brazil is hereby declared extinct from the date of this law.

Art. 2. Any provisions to the contrary are hereby revoked.

On 16 May Allen sent Nabuco his enthusiastic greetings, saying 'it is impossible for me to find the words sufficiently strong and impressive in our poor mother tongue, to convey to you the pleasure and heartfelt congratulations' that everyone wished him (I: 82). On 20 June he sent him the draft minutes of the Anti-Slavery Society committee meeting, written on parchment, containing the society's warmest congratulations (I: 86). He added that a message to the emperor had been sent through Penedo. On 8 January 1889 Nabuco told Allen that, together with André Rebouças and Gusmão Lobo, he had handed to Princess Isabel a letter of congratulations from the Anti-Slavery Society (I: 89). Nabuco commented that the Princess had performed a courageous act, adding ominously 'I trust in God she will not lose her throne for it'.[9]

After abolition

The letter from Nabuco to Allen in January 1889 is the last known letter between them until Allen wrote to Nabuco at some length in March 1899 (II: 1), even though Nabuco was twice in London for periods of nine months – from September 1890 to July 1891 and from January to September 1892. In April 1900, Allen, who in 1898 had relinquished the post of secretary he had held for almost 20 years and agreed to become honorary secretary, sent the compliments of the Anti-Slavery Society to Nabuco on his appointment as Brazilian minister in London. Or so Allen thought. This was an error, immediately corrected by Nabuco. After 10 years, the first 10 years of the Republic, devoted almost exclusively to writing, including the great three-volume biography of his father, *Um estadista do Império: Nabuco de Araújo, sua vida, suas opiniões, sua época* (1897–8), Nabuco had in fact accepted an appointment as head of a special mission to London to prepare Brazil's case in the territorial dispute with Great Britain over the boundaries of British Guiana which was due to go to arbitration by king Victor Emmanuel II of Italy (II: 6–8). Nabuco was appointed Brazilian minister in London as well as head of the special mission only in July 1900 following the sudden death of minister Souza Corrêa. The last known letter from Nabuco to Allen is dated 7 June 1900 (II: 8). On 6 March 1902 Allen wrote that both he and his brother Joseph, treasurer of the Anti-Slavery Society for 23 years, had resigned from their positions (II: 16). The reason for the break with the society, suggested in a letter of 2 April (II: 17), the last known letter from Allen to Nabuco, was the pro-Boer position adopted by the majority of the committee on the South African War. In this same letter, Allen also sent news of the second parrot Nabuco had kindly sent him in May 1899 when he heard the first had died two years earlier. The bird had bravely endured the English winter, he said, and his daughters were very fond of it. But it talked a great deal and sometime it was necessary to cover the cage to silence its shrieks. (The first parrot had died, after 10 years with the Allen family – without ever uttering a sound.)

9 The empire was in fact overthrown 18 months later on 15 November 1889.

On Charles Allen's death in December 1904 Nabuco, still minister in London (and recovering from his dismay at Victor Emmanuel's decision in favour of Britain in the British Guiana arbitration case) but preparing to go to Washington as Brazil's first ambassador to the United States, wrote to Allen's widow, Sarah E. Allen, consoling her for the loss of her husband. In this letter (III: 1) he expressed his admiration for Allen's 'burning heart' and for his dedication to the noble ideals that he had pursued throughout his life. He assured Sarah Allen that he would never forget her husband and offered to contribute to some monument in honour of his friend. Sarah replied on 12 January 1905 (III: 2). She wrote of the affection her husband had felt for Nabuco. She told him Charles had suffered from a long and painful illness, which had begun with bronchitis two years earlier. As the disease progressed, he lost the movement of both his arms but never gave up hope of recovery. In a postscript, Sarah added that the parrot was in great health. When it heard Charles's voice, it would jump up on his bed, perch on his knee and, unusually, stay very quiet. Nabuco answered Sarah on 13 January – his last letter to the Allens (III: 3). In order to cheer her up a little, but forgetting that it was the Allens' *first* parrot that had failed to speak, he told her a story about a mute parrot.

The letters

All the known letters between Nabuco and members of the British and Foreign Anti-Slavery Society were collected and included in this volume. Some between Nabuco and other British abolitionists were also included. Among the latter is the curious figure of Catherine Impey, member of the Street, Somerset branch of the equally curious International Order of Good Templars (I: 40 to 43). Also included are letters exchanged directly between the Anti-Slavery Society and the Sociedade Brasileira contra Escravidão. There are a total of 110 letters. The majority, more precisely 64 per cent, are between Nabuco and the secretary of the Anti-Slavery Society, Charles Allen. There are 29 letters from Nabuco to Allen and 42 from Allen to Nabuco. Other officers of the Anti-Slavery Society who corresponded with Nabuco were Edmund Sturge, Joseph Cooper and Travers Buxton, Allen's successor as secretary. And, finally, there are some letters to Nabuco from Joseph Alexander, a prominent member of the society's council.

The letters of Joaquim Nabuco are to be found in the archives of the Anti-Slavery Society at Rhodes House, Oxford, whose library is part of the Bodleian Library of Oxford University. Altogether there are 37 letters, including the 29 addressed to Charles Allen. Three letters sent by the Sociedade Brasileira are also part of the Rhodes House collection. One of the letters from Nabuco to Catherine Impey was found in the Wanderley Pinho archive at the Instituto

Histórico e Geográfico Brasileiro in Rio de Janeiro. A total of 71 letters from British abolitionists, including the 42 written by Allen, can be found in the Nabuco archive at the Joaquim Nabuco Foundation in Recife. One letter from Allen to the Sociedade Brasileira was taken from *O Abolicionista*.

Most of the letters are in an excellent state of repair. There were only a few cases where the original text could not be recovered. Some letters do not have a precise date but it was not difficult to attribute an approximate date. Nabuco's letters are surprisingly correct and fluent, bearing in mind that English was one of the foreign languages that he did not master so well. He sometimes asked Allen to correct his English for publication, but it was rarely necessary. However, his construction of a sentence is very Portuguese and his vocabulary often includes words from a Latin origin in place of more typically English expressions.

Some of the Nabuco-Allen correspondence was published by the Joaquim Nabuco Foundation in 1985, under the title *Joaquim Nabuco, Cartas aos abolicionistas ingleses*, edited with an introduction by José Tomas Nabuco, Joaquim Nabuco's son. Despite the merits of this publication, it includes only 23 letters, 22 from Nabuco and one from Allen. Hence the justification for this new edition that includes an additional 87 letters, fully annotated, together with a chronology, a bibliography and this introduction by the editors.

I
Correspondence 1880–9

Letter 1
Allen[1] to Nabuco (in Rio de Janeiro)

8 January 1880
55 New Broad Street, London E.C. [Offices of the British and Foreign Anti-Slavery Society]

Dear Sir

I have much pleasure in handing you the following copy of a Minute passed by the Committee of this Society.

'The Committee of the British and Foreign Anti-Slavery Society, desire to place upon record their sense of the great services rendered by Senhor Joaquim Nabuco to the cause of freedom, by the constant and untiring devotion with which he has laboured to procure the carrying out of justice towards the unfortunate Catta Branca Blacks so long held in illegal slavery by the St. John del Rey Mining Company.[2]

---

1 Charles Harris Allen (1824 or 1825–1904), Secretary of the British and Foreign Anti-Slavery Society June 1879–November 1898, honorary secretary November 1898–March 1902.

2 The St John d'El Rey Mining Company was founded in 1830. Its mine at Morro Velho in Nova Lima, Minas Gerais (near present day Belo Horizonte) was the largest gold mine in South America. The company purchased 500 slaves between 1830 and 1843 (151 in 1834 alone). See Marshall C. Eakin, *British enterprise in Brazil. The St. John d'el Rey Mining Company and the Morro Velho gold mine, 1830–1960* (Durham, NC, 1989), p. 195, Table 18. With the demise of other gold mining companies in the 1840s and 1850s – the Brazilian company (Cata Branca) 1833–44, the National Brazilian Mining Association (Cocais) 1833–46 and the Imperial Brazilian Mining Association (Gongo Soco) 1824–56 – the St John 'rented' almost 1,000 of their slaves: 385 from Cata Branca, under a contract (signed in London in June 1845) that stipulated that the adults would be freed after 14 years and the minors after 21 years; 182 from Cocais in 1861; and 400 from the creditors of Gongo Soco in the 1860s (Eakin 1989: 34). Thus in the late 1860s the St John d'el Rey Mining Company, a British company, held some 1,500 slaves. On 1 January 1868 the company freed all the children born to their own slaves as well as the Cata Branca slaves (Eakin 1989: 200). The company had always had a policy of freeing old, infirm and 'deserving' slaves on a regular basis. One hundred and ninety-nine of its own slaves were freed between 1830 and 1882, 87 of the 'rented' Cata Branca slaves between 1845 and 1879 (Eakin: 35). Others, of course, died. The British government, the British and Foreign Anti-Slavery Society from 1876, the English language press in Rio de Janeiro and, above all, in 1879 Joaquim Nabuco, recently elected to the Brazilian parliament, took up the cause of the St John d'El Rey slaves, and especially the Cata Branca slaves who under the original contract should have been freed between 1859 and 1866, and pursued their freedom (and the payment of back wages)

'The Committee have seen with pleasure the decree passed by the Juiz de Direito of the Rio das Velhas district by which the Catta Branca Blacks are now declared to be free – their freedom dating from 1860 and their wages to be allowed from that date. This Decree the Committee trust to see carried out in its entirety without delay; but meanwhile they hasten to express to Senhor Nabuco the deep sense they entertain of the manner in which he has contributed towards the end now attained, and on behalf of all the suffering slaves, they offer him their sincere thanks.

'They, also, at the same time, wish to record their sense of the services he has rendered to the cause of humanity by his vigorous attack of the Policy of the Brazilian Government in their endeavour to introduce Chinese Coolie labour under indenture into Brazil.[3] The Committee hold the opinion that this is but another name for slavery, and they trust that Senhor Nabuco will continue to oppose the introduction of so nefarious a measure; and that his efforts in this respect also, will be crowned with success.'

With the expression of my high regard
I am, Dear sir,
Yours very sincerely
Chas. H. Allen
Secretary

---

through the Brazilian and British courts. A final settlement in the case of the remaining 223 Cata Branca slaves was reached in June 1882 (see letter 31).

3 After the end of the African slave trade in the 1850s, Chinese 'coolie', indentured, immigrant labour was often proposed by Brazilian *fazendeiros* and their representatives in government and parliament as an alternative source of manpower for Brazilian agriculture. There were, however, only 436 Chinese workers registered in the Brazilian census of 1872. 1.000 were imported in 1874, but overall less than 3,000 Chinese were introduced into Brazil in the nineteenth century. See Robert Conrad, 'The planter class and the debate over Chinese immigration to Brazil, 1850–1893', *International Migration Review*, 9/1 (1975). The Chinese government was always reluctant to sanction emigration to Brazil, not least because of the notoriously harsh treatment of the Chinese in Cuba, Peru and Britain's tropical colonies. The British government was also opposed: in 1873 Chinese migration from Hong Kong was banned (except to Britain's own colonies!) and in 1874 the Portuguese authorities in Macau were persuaded to do the same. In 1878 the Sinimbu government in Brazil, the first Liberal government since 1868, was favourable to the importation of *cules*. It convoked an Agrarian Congress at which the subject was discussed, with *fazendeiro* opinion divided. At this time the Brazilian press and public were hostile to Chinese immigration, partly on ethnic or racist grounds (fears for the 'degeneration' of the Brazilian population) and partly because the traffic in coolies could become, in Joaquim Nabuco's words, 'a new slave trade' extending the life of slavery in Brazil. Nabuco had vigorously opposed the Sinimbu government on this issue in a speech in parliament on 1 September 1879.

Letter 2
Williams[4] to Nabuco

14 February 1880
Serra de Cocais, Minas Gerais

Dear Sir

I have been requested by the Secretary of the British and Foreign Anti-Slavery Society of London [Charles Allen], to forward, and which I have now the honour to do, a copy of a resolution passed by the Committee of that Society; thanking you for your successful efforts in causing the emancipation of the Catta Branca Blacks illegally held in slavery in Morro Velho; by bringing the subject under the notice of the 'Assemblea Geral'.[5]

I trust the substance of the Resolution may be as gratifying to you as it affords me pleasure in being made the means of its communication.

I am afraid there is not much chance of these Blacks receiving their wages from January 1860 to 1877 (date of deposit), unless the matter is again brought before the 'Assemblea'.

I have the honour to be
Dear Sir
Your most obedient and humble servant
Charles H. Williams

---

4 Charles Williams, director of the Cocais mines.

5 Assembléia Geral do Império, Chamber of Deputies and Senate meeting together.

Letter 3
Nabuco to Allen

8 April 1880
Rio de Janeiro

Dear Sir

I had the honour to receive the communication you kindly addressed to me [letter 1], of the Resolutions passed by the Committee of the British and Foreign Anti-Slavery Society, and I beg you to convey to your distinguished Associates, and to receive for yourself, my most sincere thanks. Your approbation was not for me a matter of doubt, therefore it honours me still more.

The fact that a great English Company has lent itself, for twenty years, to be the chief instrument for the illegal enslaving of hundreds of men, for whose freedom it had solemnly pledged itself by a public contract, could nowhere excite so much indignation as in England. It is for that that the S. João del Rey Mining Company and its accomplices had never more constant and uncompromising enemies than Her Britannic Majesty's Representatives in Brazil. I was perfectly aware then that I was rendering a service, both to the English nation and to the slaves of Morro Velho, by denouncing the spoliation of human freedom perpetrated by an important gold mining enterprise of South America under the protection of the British flag. I had only in view to call the attention of the country to that scandalous conspiracy, and give it the largest publicity. In fact justice after this step could no longer be delayed. I here must heartily join you in the praise you bestow upon the worthy magistrate, whose name I beg leave to mention, Judge Frederico Augusto Alvares da Silva, who has, by his decree, affirmed the right of the Cata Branca blacks to their freedom and salary in a way which, I am confident, will not be altered hereafter. It is unhappily much to be regretted – and it should be investigated – that out of the three hundred and eighty five slaves, who in 1845, obtained a perfect right, by a legal title, to their liberty (the minors when they should attain twenty one years, the others after fourteen years of services rendered), only one hundred and twenty three now appear to receive their letters of freedom from the hands of public justice.

As for the resistance I offered to the Chinese immigration scheme, I think with you that any labour contract celebrated in China will soon degenerate into a Slavery bond for the contracted, in whatever country he may chose to settle. I oppose the idea of sustaining artificially the large proprietorships with the Asiatic, instead of the decaying African stay. This plan meanwhile seems to meet with an insurmountable obstacle by the refusal of the Celestial Empire through its government to celebrate any treaty, allowing the emigration of its subjects to be converted into a traffic. After the fall, moreover, of the Sinimbú administration which had undertaken to furnish the agriculturers of two only of the Southern provinces with Coolies, there is no longer any reason to fear that the black be replaced by the yellow slave, and the inheritance of slave labour will appertain entirely to free people.

Thanking you once more for the gratifying message you sent me, I assure you will always find me at the fighting post I now occupy. I place the Emancipation interest beyond any other, above any party allegiance or engagement. Compared to this great social reform, which should extend the right of freedom, property, family and conscience, to the race which produces more that two thirds of Brazilian exportations, political reforms remain in the shade.

In the approaching session of the House of Deputies, besides a bill, the purport of which is to correct many of the inequalities and iniquities of the slavery covenant, I will introduce one establishing the date of the 1st of January, 1890, for the entire abolition of Slavery in the Empire.[6] I know such a large period is a compromise, but it is necessary one. It is the only means of surmounting difficulties which are still very great. The law of the 28th September, 1871, sufficient for that time, has a slower action, and gives a lower rate of yearly emancipations, than the circumstances of the country and the steady progress of public conscience, now, both allow and requires. An unchangeable term, such as the 1st of January, 1890, would leave time to the planters to prepare for the great evolution, while it would directly give rise, in the hearts of the slaves, to an invaluable hope, of an infinite price, which would render life less and less hard for them, at every step of time that should bring them nearer to freedom. This bill will not be converted this year into law; but introduced every Session in a Liberal House by myself or some of my friends, in a Conservative House by some prominent Conservative Abolitionist

6 Nabuco presented his bill on 24 August 1880. The first article read: 'On 1 January 1890 slavery will be declared abolished for all time in the territory of the empire. The State will indemnify by means of this law those who still possess slaves at that date.' Attached were the signatures of 38 deputies. Nabuco requested a decision on an early vote [*urgência na votação*]. The Liberal president of the council of ministers, José Antônio Saraiva, made it a question of confidence in the government, threatening to resign if the *urgência* were approved. The deputies supporting the government boycotted the session, depriving the chamber of the necessary quorum. Nabuco did not wish to ask for a further *urgência* but another deputy did so. The request was defeated 77 votes to 18, thus preventing discussion of the bill, which was withdrawn.

The bill was published in *O Abolicionista*, 1 January 1881, pp. 6–7 and 1 February 1881, pp. 4–5. *O Abolicionista* was the journal of the Sociedade Brasileira contra a Escravidão formed on 7 September 1880 (see letter 5). The first issue was published on 1 November 1880.

like Mr. Gusmão Lobo[7] – increasing every time in votes, it will triumph at last. As the date is immovable, every delay would render the transition period shorter, but it would not be our fault. The frontier of the next decade shall not be crossed in Brazil, I hope, by any man calling himself a slave. Such a hope I express here is sure to meet with the sympathy of the Emperor, who cannot but be earnestly desirous of leaving to his daughter a free country, rid of slavery, and who has had already forty years of reign to execute what Alexander II, of Russia, did after six, not for one million, but for forty millions of his subjects, against most terrible odds and incomparable social resistances, without disposing, in fact, of any greater strength. We will have, besides, on our side the generosity of the national character, and chiefly the complicity of the slave-owners, who out of human feelings, are actually becoming more and more the best workers of Emancipation. The law passed under Viscount of Rio Branco's administration was certainly not a compromise between two independent Sovereignties: the State and Slavery. It was not a contract, *do ut des*, nor a treaty of alliance. It was like any other, a legislative Act, to be tested by experience and by its own nature, the mere forerunner of the definitive solution. It shakened the traditional building, exposed its secular foundation, now the fall must follow. Under the last Cabinet the movement was checked for a while, but the Cabinet was thrown down and Emancipation stands. What a better signal of public spirit than the private liberality of great and small landowners, leaving, by will, all their slaves free and distributing lands amongst them? Every day a new name is inscribed in that Golden Book, whose pages every Brazilian would be proud to read. What a better signal, too, than the position assumed by the leading newspapers of the country, all favourable to Emancipation, as, for instance, the *Jornal do Comércio*, whose defence of the Redeeming Fund honours our journalism, and the *Gazeta de Notícias*, open to every social reform? All the generosity for the county is aroused, long since, in favour of progressive abolition. Anywhere, at the public meetings, as well as in the Parliament galleries every word of abolition is greeted with applause, and true popularity is attached to the memory of those who were the precursors of the idea, as well as to every statesman who tried to build the greatness of the country upon a free soil. Finally we may rely on the late, but powerful, contingent, when all those who descend from slaves will understand what a duty that legacy imposes on them towards the cause we defend. 'The fact remains, but the right has passed', said Senator Nabuco, my father, alluding to the beneficent law of the 28th of September, 1871.[8] Well, a fact that does not stand upon right, is condemned to perish; it has no internal life, and the sooner it disappears, the better.

---

7 Francisco Leopoldino Gusmão Lobo, deputy for Pernambuco.

8 The law of free birth, 28 September 1871. See Introduction.

The British and Foreign Anti-Slavery Society sees every day the propagation of its efforts. That is a result of the work of social and moral levelling, which is being carried on among civilized countries. These efforts more than once were directed towards Brazil, and they were not unsuccessful. Well, the day is not very distant, when, in the geographical map of Slavery, Brazil and Cuba, two of the most beautiful and fertile portions of the globe, will no longer be the dark spots in American land. That day, your work will be almost finished, but from that day only, a date I called the national hegira – will begin the new life of a country destined to be by the virtue of free-work alone, a blessed home, the pride of her children, born or adoptive.

Offering you the assurance of my high regard, I have the honour to be, dear Sir,
Yours very sincerely
Joaquim Nabuco
Member of the Brazilian Parliament

Letter 4
Williams to Nabuco

9 August 1880
Serra de Cocais

Dear Sir

Having been upon an excursion North far out of the way of post I have only just had the pleasure to receive you[r] letter of 24 May.[9] In the Catta Branca Slave case my latest advices from Ouro Preto, do not state that the Tribunal da Relaçao have yet given sentence in the appeal case. A note from the Minister of Justice to the President might exercise the same galvanise effect as your speech of 26 August did upon the Curador, and others at Sabará. I am most desirous for the decision, as I am anxious to withdraw my original copy of the contract which is now with the [word illegible], and which I am refused till the sentence is given and this document is necessary for the proceedings in England, against Gordon[10] and others.

I am glad to see your admirable reply to the letter of congratulations from the Anti-Slavery Society [letter 3], and your intention to introduce a Bill to enable a total end to slavery in 1890.

In the meantime, could foreigners be made subject to their own laws in regard to slavery matters?

I am progressing with the Freedom of the Blacks with whom I have to do and shortly hope to have them all free, the old ones taken care of, the young ones provided for.

I am, dear Sir
Yours very sincerely
Chas. H. Williams

9 Letter not located.

10 James Newell Gordon, superintendent of St John d'El Rey Mining Company, 1857–76.

Letter 5
Santos to Allen

8 October 1880
Rio de Janeiro,

Sir

I am directed by the Brazilian Anti-Slavery Society[11] to communicate its organisation, in Rio de Janeiro, to the British and Foreign Anti-Slavery Society.

By our 'Manifesto'[12] and the last issue of the *Rio News*, of which I have the pleasure of sending you a few copies, you will see what the purposes of our Society are, and I believe that they will meet your hearty approval.

Hoping to soon enter into direct and frequent exchange of communications with your Society on every subject relative to slavery, I have the honour to be,

Dear Sir, Your obedient servant
José Américo dos Santos
Secretary
Sociedade Brasileira contra a Escravidão

---

11 Sociedade Brasileira contra a Escravidao, founded 7 September 1880.

12 The manifesto was published in the *Gazeta de Notícias* on 28 September 1880. It appeared in English translation in the *Rio News* and in French in the *Méssager du Brésil*. Charles Allen replied on 23 November (letter 6).

Letter 6[13]
Allen to José Américo dos Santos

23 November 1880

Dear Sir

I have much pleasure, on behalf of the British and Foreign Anti-Slavery Society, in acknowledging receipt of the several copies of the Manifesto of the Sociedade Brasileira contra a Escravidão, in English, French and Portuguese. Your manifesto was received by this Society with especial pleasure, and I warmly congratulate you on having persuaded Sr Joaquim Nabuco, a member of your Chamber of Deputies, whose services on behalf of the slaves are well known to us, to be your president. Lord Granville[14] had already sent us a copy in English for our information, with a request that it be returned to him; immediately I returned it to the Secretary of State with a copy in Portuguese that you had been kind enough to send us. The manifesto was discussed at a meeting of the Society's committee on 17th inst. And a resolution of approval and congratulations was unanimously passed, a copy of which I have the satisfaction to send you. I nourish the sincere hope that the Society, which I have the honour to represent, can co-operate with your society in the task of extinguishing slavery in the shortest possible time. I will send you on a regular basis copies of the *Anti-Slavery Reporter* and, in exchange, I will be pleased to receive your own publications. The resolution mentioned above reads: It was resolved that the British and Foreign Anti-Slavery Society received with much pleasure and satisfaction the manifesto of the Sociedade Brasileira contra a Escravidão and considers the organisation of that society evident proof that slavery, as an institution, will cease to exist within a short period of time, not only in Brazil, but in all civilized countries. The British and Foreign Anti-Slavery Society, therefore, sends its warmest congratulations to the Sociedade Brasileira and expresses the hope that, through the regular exchange of information, slavery and the condition of the slaves in Brazil will become better known than hitherto by the public, both in América and in Great Britain. The contents of the manifesto are warmly approved by the society in London which will be ready at all times to collaborate with the society in Brazil in its efforts to destroy the evil that is slavery in Brazil.

Ch H. Allen
Secretary

13 This a translation into English of the Portuguese translation of Allen's letter which was published in *O Abolicionista*, 1 January 1881, pp. 3–4. The original has not been located.

14 Lord Granville, foreign secretary 1870–4 and 1880–5.

Letter 7
Sociedade Brasileira contra a Escravidão to British and Foreign Anti-Slavery Society

20 December [1880]
Rio de Janeiro,

Gentlemen

We take the liberty to inform you of the departure of the President of this Society, Deputy Joaquim Nabuco, for a few months visit in Europe, and to solicit your kind reception and your valuable assistance in any object in which we have a common interest.

The principal purpose of Mr. Nabuco's visit is to bring ourselves into more intimate relations with the societies and individuals in Europe who are interested in the extinction of the slave traffic and in the universal abolition of slavery. With such a purpose it is manifest that this principal and most important visit will be to the first and most influential organization of its kind in the world – The British and Foreign Anti-Slavery Society.

Mr. Nabuco's services, both in parliament and in the press, in [sic] behalf of the cause of abolition in Brazil have been incessant and untiring, and he stands before the country to-day as its acknowledged leader. In bespeaking your invaluable cooperation in the purposes of his visit to Europe at this time we therefore solicit not only a service which you will be pleased to render, but also a service which will be made the more efficient and valuable through its bestowal upon so prominent a leader of the anti-slavery movement in Brazil.

With the assurances of our high esteem, and of our hearty cooperation with you in your great work, we have the honour to be

Your most obedient servants
Adolpho de Barros
Vice President
José Américo dos Santos
Secretary
André Rebouças
Treasurer

Letter 8 [postcard]
Allen to Nabuco [at 32 Grosvenor Gardens, W.8]

9 February 1881
55 New Broad Street

Very glad to welcome you to England. Mr. Cooper[15] is very ill but I am going to his house this morning with your card and will write to you directly I return. Mr. Sturge[16] is also away ill. Would it be convenient for you to call here tomorrow (Thursday at 12). I am very busy with an Address to the Government and the new number of the *Reporter* or I would offer to call upon you. We should like you to sign our *two* Addresses to the Government.

C.H. Allen

15 Joseph Cooper (1800–81), honorary secretary of the Anti-Slavery Society 1871–9.

16 Edmund Sturge (1808–93), nephew of the abolitionist and founder of the Anti-Slavery Society, Joseph Sturge, secretary of the Society 1871–9 and honorary secretary since 1879 (until 1893)

Letter 9
Allen to Nabuco

14 February 1881
55 New Broad Street

Dear Sir

I have received a letter from our President Mr. Samuel Gurney[17] of Brighton, asking me to find out whether it would be convenient to you to go down to Brighton some day this week. He would like me to accompany you and he would meet us at the station and show you some of the 'lions' of that great seaside town. We should then proceed to his house to lunch and return easily to London by afternoon express.

I think Friday or Saturday would be the best time. Please let me know as soon as you can, and I will arrange which train we shall take.

When Mr. Sturge is well enough to come to town I hope we shall be able to find an opportunity for some of the older Members of this Society to meet you either somewhere in the City or at the West End.

I am much obliged for the Portuguese papers. I can read most of the report of your reception in Lisbon,[18] but unfortunately I do not know sufficient Portuguese to read your letter. Should you like any portion of it printed in our *Reporter* I shall be happy to do so if you can tell me how I can obtain it in English.

It will be too late for this month as it has now gone to press but will contain extracts from the Spanish newspaper. Next month I could print extracts from the Lisbon paper.

Meanwhile I return them to you and hope to hear that you will kindly allow me to conduct you to Brighton either on Friday or Saturday next.

I am Dear Sir
Yours very truly
Chas. H. Allen

---

17 Samuel Gurney (1816–82), banker and philanthropist, son of the abolitionist Samuel Gurney (1786–1856), president of the Anti-Slavery Society since 1864.

18 For the repercussions of Nabuco's visit to Lisbon as reported in the local press, see *O Abolicionista* 1 March 1881. The Brazilian deputy was received with full honours in the chamber of deputies on 8 January. The *Diário Popular* described him as 'tall, elegant, attractive, with extremely regular features, more like a typical Frenchman than a Brazilian'. Rafael Bordalo Pinheiro, the famous Portuguese caricaturist, offered a dinner in his honour. *The Times,* 10 January 1881, described the visit to Lisbon by the 'leader of the slavery abolition party in Brazil'.

Letter 10
Nabuco to Allen

14 February 1881
32 Grosvenor Gardens[19]

Dear Sir

I should like to write an article on the slavery question in Brazil stating all our views. I do not know if I could find the way for that article being placed before the eyes of a large member of representative people in England, by being published after correction in some Magazine of high class and influence. In case you could give me a chance of publishing it in the conditions I desire, I would begin to work in it [sic] as soon as I receive from you such assurance. I am sure no more important question could attract the attention of liberal opinion than the one on whose solution depends the fate of a whole race of men. I do not know how to write in English so as to appear before an English public, but I will have my contribution grammatically corrected by someone who knows. I think this would be a great service rendered to the emancipation cause, and that is the reason why I do not shrink before it.

If you see the possibility of any such publication, I ask you to let me know.

I saw the paragraph in the last issue of *The Economist*[20] and I thought it excellent.

I beg you to believe me, dear Mr. Allen.
Sincerely yours
Joaq. Nabuco
P.S. – I have given up the post cards. I see how easy it is to make a reputation for writing them. J.N.

---

19 Residence of the Brazilian minister in London, Francisco Inácio de Carvalho Moreira, Barão de Penedo. See the Introduction on the relations between Nabuco and Penedo.

20 Unable to locate.

Letter 11
Allen to Nabuco

3 March 1881
55 New Broad Street

My dear Senhor

The Welcome is a paper that is either owned or edited by one of our Committee. He desires me to state that if you will let him have a good photograph likeness of yourself he will have it engraved and published in his paper – together with a translation of your Madrid speech.[21] I have several copies of this speech and enclose you one herewith – as well as a copy of *The Welcome* – separately. If you would kindly let me have a *carte de visite* and a translation of the speech I will send them to the Editor of *The Welcome*. Perhaps one of the clerks in the Embassy could translate it for you as I see it is in Portuguese.

Hoping to see you tomorrow at a little after half past 4 – when our routine business will be nearly finished.

I am
Yours very truly
Chas. H. Allen

21 Nabuco gave his speech (in Portuguese) at a special session of the Sociedad Abolicionista Española held in his honour on 23 January. See *O Abolicionista*, 1 May 1881, pp. 1–4. At the end of the session Nabuco was acclaimed *socio benemérito* of the society.

Letter 12
Nabuco to Allen

Monday [March 1881]

Dear Mr. Allen

Will you be kind enough to send me a few copies of the *Reporter* in order I may send them to Brazil by to-morrow night?

I am sorry to say I do not see how I could translate my speech of Madrid busy as I am with a new unexpected work, and my friends shrink before committing themselves to write in English. I am obliged then to send you my photograph without any contribution of mine – as you kindly asked.

Wednesday or Thursday I will call at New Broad Street to see you. I remain, dear Mr. Allen,

Sincerely yours
Joaq. Nabuco

Letter 13
Cooper to Nabuco

8 March 1881
Essex Hall, Walthamstow

Dear Sir

Some time ago you were good enough to send me a card announcing your arrival in London, the receipt of which I should have acknowledged long ago, if I had not been seriously ill. So much so as to be quite unable to write to or to call upon you.

I am still a great invalid but it seems to me as if I must try to write a few lines to express my cordial regard and great respect for you – I am not able to express to you half the satisfaction with which I heard your noble manifesto read to me. It is a document which does the highest credit to you and to the Sociedade Brasileira. The principles of righteousness and justice are most ably set forth and I imagine are just what the immortal José Bonifácio[22] advocated and for which he was banished from his country more than half a century ago. I should have rejoiced if it had been in my power to unite with my colleagues in doing honour to one who is so nobly engaged in pleading the cause of the injured and oppressed. But my time in this world is drawing toward a conclusion and I am looking towards that country where the men of the earth shall no more oppress. You will not be surprised at this when I tell you that I was in my early life an humble but ardent co-adjunctor of Clarkson and Wilberforce and their fellow labourers, the pioneers in the good cause of freedom and justice.

That the blessing of the Most High and of Him who came to proclaim liberty to the captives may rest upon you and upon your labours is the desire and prayer of

Yours very sincerely
Joseph Cooper

22 José Bonifácio de Andrada e Silva (1763–1838), the 'patriarch' of Brazilian independence. He had presented to the constituent assembly of 1823 a *Representação sobre a escravatura*, later published (1825).

Letter 14
Allen to Nabuco

5 April 1881
55 New Broad Street

Dear Senhor

At the last meeting of the Committee of this Society held on the 1st April I was directed to convey to you the warm thanks of the Committee for the valuable and interesting information respecting slavery in Brazil, which you were good enough to lay before them in person at their former meeting [4 March]; and also for the excellent and exhaustive speech which you delivered at the public breakfast given by the President in your honour, on the 23rd March last at the Charing Cross Hotel.[23]

---

23 Nabuco was introduced, to an audience of 150, including 11 members of parliament, by Thomas Fowell Buxton, son of the great abolitionist Sir Thomes Fowell Buxton. Buxton had recently replaced Samuel Gurney as president of the society. The speech was published in the *Anti-Slavery Reporter* 14 April 1881 and in *O Abolicionista*, 1 June 1881, pp. 2–5.
Before reviewing the history of slavery in Brazil and the obstacles to its abolition, Nabuco addressed head-on those who attacked the abolitionists in Brazil by accusing them 'of trying to raise a sort of European moral intervention in our domestic affairs, and of disclosing to the eyes of the world a national misfortune which should be jealously hidden from view'. Brazilian abolitionists 'did not need foreign assistance owing to the absence of national help'. They had 'the strong support of almost every element of opinion which is not the partner or the client of slavery'. They fought slavery 'exactly because [they] wish to see Brazil assume a prouder position in America, by getting rid of this blot upon civilization. It is not the men who have such national sensitiveness, such a consciousness of their country's reputation abroad, that could be accused of want of patriotic reticence by those same people who for thirty years brought on us the pain of foreign interference, because they would not desist from the greed of the slave trade!' 'Emancipation in Brazil', he insisted, 'is not the creation of men who look to the approval of European feeling. Emancipation there is the natural growth on a liberal soil of the most democratic environments in America'. Nevertheless, he concluded,

> if I did not come to Europe to denounce and impeach slavery out of the court where it has a right to be judged, and will not fail to be condemned, I am only too glad when liberal opinion of any party abroad applauds our work . . . It would be as debasing for any country to govern itself according to foreign opinion, as it would be insane for it to resist its moral influences, irrespective of their origin, which always moulded its social and moral life. As Brazil has imported all the principles of her government and organization, we are not willing to build up for the first time a Chinese wall to protect

I have also the pleasure to offer you on behalf of the Committee, those other members of this Society who have had the privilege of meeting you, their warm welcome to this country and their hope that you may have a speedy and safe passage home, when you quit these shores.

I have the honour to remain
Dear Senhor
Yours most sincerely
Chas. H. Allen

---

slave holders from the general influences which have made the world incompatible with slavery.

The speech was given extensive coverage in the London press. The reporter from *The Times* observed that it was 'rather too long'. The *Evening Standard* commented that it was given 'in excellent English'. Besides *O Abolicionista*, the *Jornal do Comércio*, the most respected newspaper in Brazil, which maintained a correspondent in London, reported the coverage of the English newspapers.

Letter 15
Nabuco to Allen

Thursday
[April 1881]

Dear Mr. Allen

I have received the kind communication you made to me [letter 14] of the approval of your Society to the speech I delivered at the Charing Cross at breakfast [23 March] and I only can repeat to you that I leave England under great obligations towards every person connected with the 'Anti Slavery'. I will try to put myself in correspondence with you, in whom I have met more than with a sympathiser of the abolition cause, with a good friend. I will leave for Brazil by the steamer of the 20th from Bordeaux. Everything was arranged for my leaving England on the 9th but now I feel it is impossible to leave so soon, and I will only start early next week for Paris, without any hope of being able to stay in Lisbon longer than a few hours. Next week I will go and see you at the Anti-Slavery office and say goodbye. I wish you kindly tell Mrs. Allen how much I did appreciate her kindness to me.

If it were possible, I would go to-morrow by 3 o'clock to New Broad Street 55, but I am afraid I will be too busy with my engagements.

Will you be kind enough to let me have the full report of the breakfast even if it is in proofs of the *Reporter* so that I may send it to-morrow evening by the Southampton mail to Brazil?

I went last week to see you, but unfortunately you were occupied with the Boers.[24]

Believe me always, dear Mr. Allen,
Truly yours
Joaq. Nabuco

---

24 A reference to the First Boer War (1880–1). The British had captured the Cape Colony from the Dutch in 1806. The Boers were the descendents of the (mainly Dutch) settlers of the East Cape frontier in South Africa who in the 'Great Trek' from 1835 to 1837 escaped British rule and formed the republics of Orange Free State, Transvaal and Natal. After several decades of conflict the republics were annexed by the British Crown following the second Boer War (1899–1902).

Letter 16
Cooper to Nabuco

15 April 1881
Essex Hall, Walthamstow

My dear friend

I feel exceedingly obliged for the excellent portrait which you have so kindly sent me.

I need scarcely say that it will be much valued by my family and by myself for as long as I remain here. It will always remind me of your able and fearless advocacy of the rights of the downtrodden and oppressed, and although I cannot expect ever to meet again in this world, may we meet around the throne in that great company whose robes have been washed and made white in the blood of the Lamb.

Always think of me as sincerely and cordially yours
Joseph Cooper

Letter 17
Nabuco to Allen

5 June 1881
Rio de Janeiro

Dear Mr. Allen

I arrived here a month ago, but so many engagements and duties were waiting for me that only now can I write to you and think of the pleasure which your acquaintance gives me. I have nothing new to tell you about the anti-slavery here. I was well and warmly received by my friends, but I doubt if the reception I met with in Europe has not been a fine subject for the pro-slavery party to play with before the Constituencies. It is current that this House will be dissolved and new elections will by all means take place this year. I present myself now for Rio de Janeiro, the Capital of the Empire, and a strong work will be done on my side. The result appears very doubtful, Rio being a very important point for both parties, to win which is by itself a victory greatly coveted. If I lose my seat in Parliament I will have had a very short political career, but I will be glad not to have a long one by submitting to slavery and treating with it. I send you one of the portraits you wish for and the other three to the person whose names are written on the back, praying you to forward them to their addresses. I present my respects to Mrs. Allen and hope to be able to see her often if by any means I leave public life by a contrary vote of this city. In this case I will do my best to spend some time in England, helping from London as much as I can the abolitionist movement here. The next elections are all important for us, because the question can only be decided in Parliament.

Emancipation cannot be done through a revolution, which would be to destroy everything – it will only be carried by a Parliamentary majority – and therefore it is for us a great question not to become a still smaller minority than we were.

Believe me, dear Mr. Allen,
Truly yours
Joaq. Nabuco

Letter 18
Nabuco to Allen

13 June 1881
Rio de Janeiro

My dear Mr. Allen

Will you be kind enough to forward the enclosed letter to Sr. Regidor Jurado,[25] whose address I forgot? I have not received news from yourself since I arrived here, but hope they are at present crossing the sea. I am sorry I left England before the Season when there was hardly anything for me to do here. I remain my dear Mr. Allen,

Sincerely yours,
Joaq. Nabuco

25 Letter not found. Recipient unidentified.

Letter 19
Nabuco to Allen

23 October 1881
Rio de Janeiro

Dear Mr. Allen

I have only time to write to you a short letter to let you have the decision of our Supreme Court on the 'Morro Velho' case. The sentence of the Ouro Preto Court of Appeal has been annulled and the appeal Court of Rio shall give a new judgement on the point to the black wages and their right to freedom by force of the 1845 contract. The importance of the *Acordão* which ordered the revision of the Minas sentence is chiefly that by the Ouro Preto sentence the blacks were considered free by the Morro Velho's concession of freedom in 1880 and not by the 1845 contract, while the Supreme Court says that their right to freedom dates from the contract between the Catta Branca and the Morro Velho Companies in that year. It is very important too that it was proposed in the Supreme Court to bring over official proceedings against the Morro Velho for having reduced free people, *of whose freedom they were conscious,* to slavery by matriculating them in 1872 as slaves. Such was the vote, as you will see in the Acordão, of the Ministers of the Supreme Court Silveira e Sayão Lobato. The court did not vote the criminal proceedings simply because they do not technically consider to be the same crimes of reducing free people to slavery when the people are *actually* free and when they only have however clear and *incontestable* a right to freedom. This is a purely technical ground and does not signify that the Ministers who voted against the prosecution hold any different view from their colleagues, who pressed for it on the point of the conspiracy and the *keeping* in slavery of men who ought to be *freed* twenty two years ago.

On the 31st the electoral battle shall be decided and it is almost impossible for me to win. The candidate who will probably defeat me is himself a *fazendeiro* (coffee planter) in S. Paulo. I present myself in Rio – it was a very bold attempt to struggle with slavery in the city, they pretend to be the coffee capital. If I am defeated, as I expect, I will probably go to London for a few years, as I can hardly do anything out of Parliament except to educate the people by pamphlets and writing and this I can do better in London than here. The greatest suffering of the position I took is that I can do nothing to help the poor slaves who every day come to be believing I have power to free them, while I can only send them back to the slavery quarters and to their master's wrath. I will send to you the documents of the campaign and the results of the vote. I intend saying in my next address that if I am defeated I will bear proscription and the social antagonism which their vote of ostracism shows to exist between the abolitionists and the electors, with the same resignation and patience with which the slaves bear their intolerable condition. In a country where over one million of men have no rights whatever, neither to have a family protected by law or property of their own except with great risk – nor to have their labour payed [sic] at least one day during their lives – it is a very mild sentence that which may condemn me to leave political life and my seat in Parliament to the slave owners and the delegates of slavery. I beg you, my dear friend, to remember me kindly to Mrs Allen, to present my warm wishes for his health to the venerable Mr. Cooper and to present my compliments of fellow worker and associate to Mr. Gurney, Mr. Sturge and Mr. Crawford.[26] I am always

Sincerely yours
Joaq. Nabuco

P.S. – What a grand work you have done in Egypt![27] I was to write a short note and I came to this page. Pardon me. J.N.

---

26 Joseph Crawford, former consul-general in Havana, member of the committee of the Anti-Slavery Society.

27 The Anti Slavery Society was involved in the struggle for the abolition of the domestic slave trade and domestic slavery in Egypt.

Letter 20
Allen to Nabuco
22 November 1881

55 New Broad Street.

My dear Senhor

I was very pleased to receive your friendly letter of 23rd Oct [letter 19] and hasten to reply to it.

The Portuguese version of the decision of the Court in the 'Morro Velho' case has been forwarded to the Solicitors of the Treasury. I am very glad to tell you that this case is now very nearly ripe for prosecution in the English Courts and I hope you will shortly hear something about it. *But this is strictly in confidence.* Thank you very much for you[r] kind interest and assistance in the matter.

We are anxiously awaiting the result of your great electoral contest – and quite hope you will be returned for Rio de Janeiro. Should however the powers of evil be too strong and you should be compelled to allow them to ride over your head – *for a season* – how gladly we shall *all* welcome you back to England. You will certainly be able to aid the good cause very much by your eloquent voice which will be heard across the wide Atlantic and will give courage and strength to the poor slave! By this mail I send you a copy of the [Parliamentary] Slave Papers No.1 1881 which please accept from us. They contain interesting matters relating to Brazil, which you will see we have noticed in the last Reporter [November 1881]. There will be also a short further notice in the next number. Mr. Sturge is very well and desires to be kindly remembered to you – also Mr. Crawford. Poor Mr. Cooper will hardly survive this winter I think. He seems fast breaking up. Mrs. Allen is well and desires her kindest regards. She is now at Oxford as my youngest son has gone there to try and win a scholarship. The eldest is at Cambridge studying mathematics etc.

I am glad you approve our work in Egypt. It is still far from finished – but we hope to obtain freedom for the Slave someday and I trust you will see the same for your million and a half enslaved human beings in Brazil.

With best wishes I am ever yours very sincerely
Chas. H. Allen

Letter 21
Nabuco to Allen

2 January [1882]
32 Grosvenor Gardens.

Dear Mr. Allen

Here I am back again, wishing to remain for a couple of years studying English institutions and making the best use of my stay abroad. I will see you this week in your office – but I do not know on what day.

I send you the portrait you wished for – and a number of the 'Abolitionist' started after my departure.[28] When we meet we shall talk about so many things.

Sincerely yours
J. Nabuco

28 *O Abolicionista*, in its last issue, 1 December 1881, reported Nabuco's departure for London that day, banished from parliament 'thanks to the hatred and envy of those who considered him an invincible athlete [sic]', and included the text of his farewell address 'To the Abolitionists of Brazil' on withdrawing from the country 'temporarily'. The report (in which 'atleta invencível' was translated as 'dangerous antagonist') and Nabuco's 'bold and manly' address as he began his 'virtually enforced exile' were reprinted in the *Anti-Slavery Reporter*, February 1882.

Letter 22
Allen to Nabuco

3 January 1882
55 New Broad Street.

My dear Senhor

[Greeting illegible] or One hundred thousand welcomes to the friendly though foggy shores of Old England! I hope you are quite well after your long voyage and your hard fight in the cause of freedom. I shall be very glad to see you once more. Mr. Sturge wishes me to invite you to our next Committee – on Friday the 6th inst. at 4.30. Will you come? If not send me a card saying *when* I may expect you, so that I may not be out. I believe I am going to the South of France next week for a month and therefore I do not wish to miss you. I hope you will come to the Committee. As you are a corresponding Member you have the right to attend every month.

Many thanks for the photograph. It is an admirable likeness. I want to make an Anti-Slavery Album for the Office.

Mrs. Allen will be very glad to hear of your safe arrival and when I return from Menton I hope you will honour us with your company. We live where we did. My children are well. The eldest boy is at Cambridge (not *now* as it is vacation). The younger has just won a scholarship at Balliol College – Oxford – the greatest university prize there is for beginners. He is only 17½ so that the honour is the greater.

Ever yours very sincerely
Chas. H. Allen
Secretary

I send you a memorial card of dear Mr. Cooper.
Thanks for *O Abolicionista.*
I should like to print your address [see note to letter 21 above] next month.

Letter 23
Nabuco to Allen

Thursday [January 1882]
19 Brook Street

Dear Mr. Allen

I am very busy to day and therefore could do no better than what I include.

I have not yet my papers in order, and so I could not find the date of the sentence of the Court of Appeal which I suppose was delivered in November 1880, nor the date of the Supreme Court sentence which occurred by the end I suppose too of October 1881, nor the date in which the last Sentence by the Revising Provincial Court appointed by the Supreme Court is to be pronounced, nor finally if this last Court is that of Rio or that of S. Paulo. The last two points I could find in the letter of Mr. Jacintho Dias da Silva[29] written lately to me if I knew where I put it – and the two first in the *Rio News*.

I saw your note to-day in *The Times*. Unhappily I was writing to you about Mr. Morrison's doings and only now someone reads to me in *The Times* that he died in London a few days ago.[30] I am very sorry for it, as he probably did not know how to extricate the Company from 20 years of guilt. Truly yours

Joaq. Nabuco

29 Lawyer for the Cata Branca slaves. See letter 25.

30 Pearson Morrison, company secretary, St John d'El Rey Mining Company, sent out to Morro Velho in 1876 to replace James Newell Gordon as superintendent and clean up the affairs of the company.

Letter 24
Nabuco to Allen

5 January 1882
St James Club, Piccadilly

Dear Mr. Allen

I am so very busy today and tomorrow that I must deprive myself of the great pleasure of going to the City in order to see you until the end of the week. Next week you say you are going to France. Well when you come back I shall see you. Now we have plenty of time. I am very sorry not to be able to be present to the meeting of the Committee tomorrow – but I hope on the next months to renew my acquaintance with that worthy body and see again Mr. Sturge. Unhappily I did not arrive in time to pay my last respects to poor Mr. Cooper.[31] He lived a noble life – that is the best one can do. Give my compliments to your sons for the pleasure they are causing you and please represent my respects to Mrs. Allen.

Good bye and *au revoir*
Truly yours
J. Nabuco

31 Joseph Cooper died in December 1881.

Letter 25
Nabuco to Sturge

23 January 1882
19 Brook Street.

Dear Mr. Sturge

As Mr. Allen is now in the south of France, I take the liberty of troubling you to get some information on a point which does interest you so much, the Morro Velho Company's case about the slaves it has illegally held. The representative of the Blacks against the Morro Velho Company wants to know: 1°. – If it exists in London any representation of the extinct Catta Branca Company and if it does where does it function and what are its character, powers and legal standing; 2°. – If between the representatives of the Catta Branca Company, if such exist, and the Morro Velho Company is there any union or community of interests known in the City; 3°. – Who are those persons, what is their public character, and their social position or profession.

Mr. Jacintho Dias da Silva, who pleads the cause of the Blacks, now in appeal before the Relação, writes to me to have that information, which he says he asked too from the British Legation in Rio, and finds very useful and almost necessary for the stating of the Blacks rights as the Morro Velho insists in having paid the salaries to the extinct Catta Branca's delegates. I am sure you know all about it and could give me the information Mr. Dias da Silva wants to embody in his defence of the poor slaves' right. I am sorry to trouble you, and am ready to call on you at the Anti-Slavery Room to get the necessary information.

I wish you every prosperity. Believe me, dear Mr. Sturge,
Respectfully yours
Joaquim Nabuco

Letter 26
Allen to Nabuco

21 February 1882
55 New Broad Street

My dear Senhor

I was so surprised to hear from you yesterday that Mr. Kingdon[32] has made you so insulting and flagrant a proposition as to commission that I took the opportunity this morning of letting him know that you did not think of employing him as your printer. Without telling him anything of what passed I let him understand that you were somewhat annoyed, and he immediately guessed the reason. He then explained to me exactly what he had really proposed and intended and said he had feared afterwards from your manner that you quite misunderstood him. Mr. Kingdon besides being a printer is what is called a Commission Merchant or Agent – a well known most respectable business – and one in which I was once largely engaged myself in connection with Australia.

Mr. K. has lived many years in Madagascar where he taught the natives in the Government press the art of printing. Many of his friends in that Island and in South Africa send him orders to buy goods not only for printing but for all sorts of purposes. These are of course accompanied with a remittance. He buys the goods and ships them out with the invoice – to which he adds *openly* and above board the usual commission for trouble of 5 per cent or whatever may be agreed on. On hearing from you that you were thinking of taking an Office in the City he thought you were going to start as Commission Merchant with Brazil – and the idea immediately occurred to him that he could buy all things connected with printing better than you could yourself – and that he would willingly buy these for you and divide the commission, as your agent. This is very often done by Merchants where one is better qualified than another to act as buyer – and it makes no difference to the principal who is of course only charged one commission of 5 per cent.

Now this is a totally different thing from offering a commission as a bribe – where the price is added on and charged to the principal *as part of the price*, – which is gross deception. Mr. Kingdon utterly repudiates such transactions as this and says he has never paid one sixpence of commission to anyone in his life and never would – although I know he received a hint in your Embassy that this was the only way to get business! Mr. Sturge and I have known Kingdon

32 Abraham Kingdon was the printer of the *Anti-Slavery Reporter* and in August 1883 of Nabuco's book *O Abolicionismo.*

for some time and have always had the highest opinion of him – nor do we believe he would ever stoop to such a method of obtaining business. I enclose two testimonials of his which you will do well to read. So well have I thought of him that I have more than once advanced him money to carry on his business – and indeed have some now not been paid.

When I see you next I can explain more fully what I may have only poorly expressed in this letter. What day next week will suit you to pay us a friendly visit and dine *en famille* with us? Will Thursday or Friday be convenient?

Yours very sincerely
Chas. H. Allen

Letter 27
Sturge to Nabuco

24 February 1882
Devonshire House Hotel, Bishopsgate Without

Dear Mr Nabuco

I inclose [sic] a draft of an 'interpellation' [sic] for one of our friends to make in the House of Commons.

Before doing so we should be glad to have your views upon it, or any suggestion or any alteration you may think should be made in it.

Believe me
Yours very truly
Edmund Sturge

Letter 28
Nabuco to Allen

[June 1882]
19 Brook Street

Dear Mr. Allen

Can you put into English, or translate it into English, the article I send you for the *Reporter*,[33] or make an article of your own upon it.

I have sent to my friends in Rio a petition to be signed by them, already signed by me and my friend Admiral Costa Azevedo, who is staying in London, and I will ask you to publish it in the *Reporter* next month. Meanwhile I will think of the English address – and then ask you to help me to do something in the United States through Mr. F. [Frederick] Douglass.[34]

I have so much to do, unhappily, that I really [do not] have any spare time left to write on my favourite subject, of abolition, but I have a strong desire to write a full paper on slavery in Brazil for some magazine and one in French for the *Rappel* which Mr. Schoelcher[35] says to me would insert it.

Next week I will go and see you and Mr. Sturge. I wish you to present my respects to Mrs. Allen.

Very truly yours
J. Nabuco

33 Unable to locate.

34 Frederick Douglass (1818–95), freed American slave, one of the leaders of the abolitionist movement in the United States.

35 Victor Schoelcher (1804–93), who as president of the French abolitionist committee had played a major role in the abolition of slavery throughout its colonies by France in 1848.

Letter 29
Nabuco to Allen

21 June 1882
19 Brook Street

Dear Mr. Allen

Thanks for the *Reporter*. I send you wishing you could correct it when you have any leisure, for insertion in some *future* number of your paper, the petition which I sent to Brazil to be signed there by our friends. To-morrow or the day after I will go to the City and talk to you. I did not go last week on account of having much to do.

Believe me always,
Very truly yours,
Joaquim Nabuco

Letter 30
Nabuco to Allen

Saturday [June/July 1882]
19 Brook Street

Dear Mr. Allen

I send you the original of the petition I sent to our Parliament.[36] The paragraphs numbered are the only ones which ought to be translated, the others having not been included in the address.

In the next number of the *Reporter* I will write something on Brazilian topics.

Ever yours truly,
J. Nabuco

36 The petition, signed in London on 4 June by Nabuco and Rear Admiral José da Costa Azevedo, was presented to the chamber of deputies by Antônio Pinto, deputy for Ceará, on 14 July, Bastille Day. It demanded 'the total emancipation of the slaves, immediately or within a short term, to be defined at the time'. See *Anães do Parlamento Brasileiro*, 1882 tomo II, p. 294. The text was also published in the *Jornal do Comércio* on 15 July. It appeared in English translation in the *Anti-Slavery Reporter*, August 1882.

Letter 31
Nabuco to Allen

16 July 1882
19 Brook Street

Dear Mr. Allen

I must congratulate you and the Anti-Slavery on the final sentence delivered against the Morro Velho Company and in favour of the Blacks.[37] I enclose the article of the 'Rio News' of the 24th which I dare say you have seen wishing you if you have another copy to return me the scrap.

This week I will go and see you and talk about Brazilian matters unless you write to me that you shall not be in your office either on Wednesday or Thursday next.

Please present my compliments to Mr. Sturge and believe me always
Very truly yours
Joaq. Nabuco

37 Judgement of the Brazilian 'final court of appeal' (Supremo Tribunal de Justiça), 22 June 1882, published in English translation in the *Anti-Slavery Reporter* August 1882. For the history of the Cata Branca slaves, see notes 1 and 2.

Letter 32
Allen to Nabuco

21 July 1882
55 New Broad Street

My dear Sir

I was talking to Mr. Sturge about what you said in reference to the probability of the Catta Branca slaves being induced on payment of £10 or £20 to sign a release in full of all claim for back wages!

Mr. Sturge thinks there ought to be someone appointed to protect these poor Blacks if possible. If it were in England the money would be ordered to be paid into Court – so as to be safe and properly administered. We do not know what course is adopted in Brazil, but it is important some security should be found so as to ensure the payment of the sums due. Mr. Sturge thinks that possibly you might be able to write out by the mail of the 24th to call the attention of some qualified person to this matter. Probably he would be at some expence [sic] in postage and telegraphic messages or fees to court messengers and I am therefore authorized to say that you may draw upon this Society to any amount not exceeding £10 (ten pounds) for such expenses.

Will you kindly give this your thought and let me know what you advise and also whether the steps necessary for protection of the Blacks can be taken.

We shall possibly get a question asked in the House of Commons about the Cocais Co. and the Court of Chancery.

Mrs. Allen hopes you can fix some day next week after Tuesday to come and see us.

Yours very truly
Chas. H. Allen

Letter 33
Nabuco to Allen

7 August [1882]
19 Brook Street

Dear Mr. Allen

I send you the extract such as it appeared in the *Jornal do Comércio* [15 July – see letter 30] of Sr. Antonio Pinto on introducing my petition to Parliament.

Are you coming down to the City at all this week? I would like very much to see you then.

Truly yours
Joaq. Nabuco

Letter 34
Nabuco to Sturge

16 August 1882
Malvern Lodge, Norfolk Square, Brighton

Dear Mr. Sturge

I send you confidentially, wishing you to send it back to me after reading, a letter I received last year on the subject of certain blacks in Minas Gerais, as you might talk to the persons concerned in the case and see what to do in favour of the slaves.

I do not think Mr. Allen is in town, if he is with you please show him the letter.

Very truly yours
Joaq. Nabuco

P.S. I read in *The Times* that the Institute of International Law is to meet in Turin on the 11th Sept. next. I think before the Institute some *memorandum* ought to be read asking for a public condemnation of slavery in the name of international law by the Institute. If necessary, I could send you a petition as I should like to sign it for the Anti Slavery of Rio de Janeiro. I think some prominent Englishman belongs to the Institute and could take charge of the case. I can send you a *memorandum* of the points on which the petition must stand. I can have the document ready on the 30th August so as to give you ample time to have it forwarded to Turin before the Institute meets. I know it is fully in the scope of the Institute to consider the matter from an international, pacific and civilising point of view.
J.N.

Letter 35
Sturge to Nabuco

18 August 1882
Charlbury, Oxfordshire

Dear Sen Nabuco

Your letter of the 16th [letter 34] with the enclosed reaches me here.

Our Secretary is now away in Switzerland and will not return for fully three weeks.

The story of the Blacks held by the company of which Samuel Gurney Sheppard is the Chairman is an old one. We can talk about it when the Secretary returns, and we next have the pleasure of seeing you.

I thank you for your mention of the International Law Congress. I will write at once to a member of our Committee who has sometimes attended them with a view to the carrying out of your suggestion.

Please inform me when you leave Brighton and where your future address will be.

Meanwhile
Yours truly
Edmund Sturge

On further consideration, I think it important that such a document as you propose should go to the Congress, and I will ask you to prepare it at once. I am writing to the Secretary on the subject. It has a special importance just now in that when the powers of Europe meet in conference vis the *final* settlement in Egypt the slave trade question must be considered.[38]

38 The British had invaded and occupied Egypt in August–September 1882, making it a de facto British protectorate.

Letter 36
Sturge to Nabuco

26 August 1882
Charlbury, Oxon

Dear Sen Nabuco

Since I wrote to you last week I have seen my friend and colleague Mr. J.G. Alexander. He has been in communication with Sir Travers Twiss[39] who is considered to be the most influential of the English members of the International Law Conference. Sir Travers considers the subject to be one of very great importance, but from having been unwell lately is doubtful of being able to give it full consideration.

Mr. Alexander was intending to visit Brighton at this time, and I hope will see you.

Yours very truly
Edmund Sturge

39 Sir Travers Twiss QC (1809–97) was president of the International Law Association in 1883.

Letter 37
Nabuco to Sturge

28 August 1882
Brighton

Dear Mr. Sturge

I have just received your letter [letter 36] on the subject I wrote to you about, and I am very sorry to hear that Mr. Travers Twiss could not place the point before the body in which he is so influential.

I am sure the International Law Conference you speak of was not meant by you to be the Conference for the reform of the International Law which met in Liverpool, but the *Institut de Droit International* which is to meet in Turin on Sept. the 11th.

I was preparing a paper on 'Slavery before the International Law' – but as you cannot have the subject conveniently brought before the *Institut*, it is better to postpone it to the meeting of next year. Meanwhile I will enlarge the paper I was writing and make it more complete when I go to London, as I have no books here.

Believe me always very truly yours
Joaq. Nabuco

Letter 38
Alexander[40] to Nabuco

17 September 1882
Roxburghe
Sandown, Isle of Wight,

Dear Senhor Nabuco

Enclosed I forward, as promised, [a] copy of my paper on the Slave Trade, and our report on the Berlin Congress.[41] You will see that our declaration no. 2 is Bluntschli's article in another form.[42]

I wrote to Mr. Sturge on Friday, as he was not in London when I was there last week, and told him what I thought necessary. My programme of measures to be urged upon our Government is fourfold – the two declarations are recommended, (3) an international arrangement for a mixed commission at Zanzibar to try cases arising out of the Slave Trade, with the needful provisions as to the right of search, (4) that England should assist the Khedive's Government[43] in enforcing the prohibition of the land traffic through the Sudan and Upper Egypt, so that the prohibition becomes a reality. It seems to me that these measures, if vigorously carried out by our Foreign Office, would suffice to put an end to the East African slave trade in a very short time – though it might be desirable afterwards to follow them up by placing a light draught cruiser on Lake Tanganyika.

Of course all this would only have an indirect influence on the Brazilian question, but I should think the moral influence on Brazilian opinion must, as you have said, be great.

I have proposed to Mr. Sturge the following means of carrying out these objects. First, a manifesto to be issued by the Anti-Slavery Society, appealing to our countrymen to support us in urging upon our Government to take advantage of the present magnificent opportunity to carry out the above programme – I have since drawn up such a manifesto. Secondly, that public meetings be organized in our principal towns during the latter part of October,

40 Joseph Alexander, member of the committee of the Anti-Slavery Society.

41 Convened by Bismarck in 1878, the congress of Berlin brought together the European Great Powers primarily to discuss the crisis in the Balkans.

42 Johann Caspar Bluntschli (1808–81), Swiss international lawyer, one of the founders of the Institute of International Law. Article not identified.

43 Khedive was the title of the rulers of Egypt and the Sudan belonging to the dynasty created by Muhammad Ali Pasha which lasted from 1805 to 1914. In 1882 Great Britain invaded Egypt in support of its ally the Khedive Tawfiq (1879–92), son of Ismail Pasha (1863–79).

at which I have said you and I are willing to attend as a deputation. I have also mentioned that I propose writing an article for the *Nineteenth Century*, and that you intend writing to *The Times*. I will let you know what Mr. Sturge says when I have his reply.

Yours very truly.
Joseph G. Alexander

Sept. 18. This morning I have Mr. Sturge's reply approving the idea of a manifesto, but saying nothing about meetings.

Letter 39
Allen to Nabuco

25 October 1882
55 New Broad Street

Dear Sir

This Society has arranged to hold a Public Meeting at Willis' Rooms, King St, St James', on Wednesday the 15th of Nov. at 3 p.m. (the Rt Hon. the Earl of Shaftesbury K.G. in the chair) in order to consider the present favourable opportunity for procuring the abolition of Slavery and the Slave Trade in Egypt.

The Committee invite your cordial cooperation, and will be glad if you will kindly consent to speak at the meeting in favour of the above object.

An early answer will oblige
Yours sincerely
Chas. H. Allen

I hope you are quite well and will be able to give us a good speech on the 15th. When are you coming to the City? C.H.A.

Letter 40
Catherine Impey to Nabuco

20 November 1882
I. O. G. T. [International Order of Good Templars]
Temperance Mission
Street
Somerset

Dear Signor Nabuco

You will not forget your kind promise to write a letter to our meeting on Monday next. I wish you could be persuaded to come and read it in person – I wish you could set aside business claims for one evening and plead the rights of the coloured men – those in your own country. Come and speak of the *sin* of keeping men in slavery merely because they are too helpless to resist.

Join us in proclaiming that the coloured man should have a fair chance in life – that his rights should be respected, his life sacred, his wife and children and his home – his own.

The ticket I enclose is a 'proof' only. They are printing on the others that a written address from *you* is part of the programme.

We would put you to no expense – except that of your time and presence – Can you not come.

Very truly yours
Catherine Impey

Letter 41[44]
Nabuco to Impey

24 November 1882
London

Dear Miss Impey

I am very sorry not to be able to join those who will give you their hearty support on Monday next, but I wish to assure you of the deep sympathy with which I heard you speak of the struggle being carried on against the *prejudice of colour*. It is certainly a spot which cannot pass unnoticed in the bright aspects of American democracy that there the negro races find in the colour of their skin unsurmountable [sic] obstacles to social equality and full citizenship, however pure, noble and unselfish their representatives may be. This repulsion has outlived slavery, in fact while it exists slavery cannot be said to have entirely died out. The 'Life of Frederick Douglass' shows almost in every page what a struggle a coloured man would have in the Union to make people forget his colour, look at his character and not his race and admire his eloquence without being ashamed of his company. What is called now in England *boycotting* had been, morally and socially, the fate of the whole negro race in America, and if slavery broke materially that barrier and the negroes were not left altogether alone it was because their unpaid services were too precious. Intercourse never went beyond the interests of the cotton crop.

I know that in no country whatever are there so many intellectual and progressive forces in activity as in North America, and I feel sure that six millions of Americans, as the negroes are now, will find strong and universal support to wage war against colour prejudice and to carry it from the law, in whose territory it is already won, into all the departments of Church and State, of administration and learning, into the whole field of trade, industry and general social intercourse, only to stop at the line of aristocracy, too exclusive and limited to be governed except by its own code of rank and prejudice.

As for Brazil, my own country and home, I can only repeat here what I told you: even with slavery we make no difference as to colour. Coloured men happen to be foremost in all careers: none is shut to them either by law or by public antipathy or social pressure. Some of the most brilliant talents, in all kinds of intellectual superiority, come from the coloured people. Poets, musicians, orators, engineers, publicists, statesmen, show us how we should have deprived ourselves of real national forces, if we had condemned, by a law,

44 This letter is from the Wanderley Pinho archive, Instituto Histórico e Geográfico Brasileiro (IHGB), Rio de Janeiro.

or still worse – by a prejudice, a whole race to live in an inferior level to our own and not to aspire to the same pursuits, achievements and ambitions in life!

No doubt can be entertained about the capacity, either intellectual or moral, of coloured people to help in the work of European civilization and add to it if properly educated and treated. It was only slavery that deprived the children of the negroes, born in America, as it degraded during the time of the Romans the Slavonic nation who gave its name for ever to the men held in property, as it was another kind of slavery, political despotism, that degraded the proudest races of the world until manliness, self-respect and personal dignity passed as distinctive qualities from the descendents of the Athenians and Romans to the descendents of their slaves.

Well, if it is slavery that degraded the negro races in America, it is freedom that will rehabilitate them, or if they prove by an infinite number of everyday examples that they are capable, very eager and thirsty of progress, if they are not like the Asiatic, bound to an immovable past, nor like the savages to the wild and erratic instincts of an earlier human period, but, on the contrary, willing to work in the line and for the aims of European influence and action, the colour prejudice which tends to keep those races backward, to hinder their advance and frustrate their efforts to self culture, is an injustificable wrong done them, a true persecution, such as is possible in the XIXth century and a cruel oppression of which they may be the sufferers, but of which the white people remain before history the inflicters.

Believe me, dear Miss Impey,
Yours truly,
Joaquim Nabuco

Letter 42
Impey to Nabuco

28 December 1882
I.O.G.T. Temperance Mission
Street
Somerset

Dear Señor Nabuco

What can you have thought of my long silence, in return for the great kindness with which you have treated me! Your letter [letter 41] reached me safely and in good time and was deeply appreciated by those of us who were setting up that meeting in Bristol. We felt ourselves a small and somewhat insignificant hand in the eyes of the public, and though we were very much in earnest we were none of us very 'gifted'.

Your excellent letter seemed to say with *weight* – many things which peculiarly wanted saying – Especially I liked the way you showed how *nations* suffer by limiting the aspirations of any particular class. And when you tell what coloured men *unfettered* have done in Brazil you prove most forcibly that the reason coloured men are not great in the Union is for lack of opportunity – not from lack of talent.

I have been anxious to give your letter wider circulation as I know there are many who would read it thoughtfully if it were before them – but in my great care (!) of the original copy I unintentionally sent it with other papers in an envelope to one of my London friends, and could not for weeks discover its whereabouts. It did not for a long time occur to me what had become of it and we spent hours in looking through every drawer or desk where it seemed possible it might be, and of course in vain, I kept on deferring my letter to you hoping it might turn up and I cannot tell you the satisfaction it gave me to one day receive it again by post.

I find myself wanting to know more about Brazil and your slaves and your social life etc. If you know any good book in English – that would give me a fair notion of what life in Brazil is like at the present time – I should be greatly obliged by you naming it—Unfortunately I have but little time for reading – life is a very busy affair with me but when a book comes in my way bearing in any special way upon the question of slavery or the condition of the Negro race – I somehow make time to read it. I want to know what the efforts of your own Anti-Slavery Society are directed to. What class of people you secure to your movement – what your modes of work – whether you wish to buy off those who still remain in slavery – or whether you are trying to enlighten public feeling and public opinion until people shall voluntarily free their slaves. Do free coloured men ever hold slaves?

But do not answer me if a book will do. I feel you have been very generous of your time already and that I ought to be ashamed to ask more.

With warmest thanks and many apologies for my incivility
I am very truly yours
Catherine Impey. (You notice our seal or stamp?)

Letter 43
Impey to Nabuco

24 April 1883
Temperance Mission
Street
Somerset

Senhor J. Nabuco

Dear Sir

I want to trouble you with a question which sometimes perplexes me. People say 'prejudice against colour is dying out – therefore why attempt any fresh efforts? Let well alone' etc. etc. etc.

It struck me today that you must have thought this matter out and could perhaps help me to answer it, and I feel sure that for the sake of the oppressed whom I am *trying* to help, you will be willing to help me and will forgive me for troubling you. With you – in Brazil – I understand that slavery is being gradually abolished. The *children* are to be free after they become 21 years old. Why do you not sit down and quietly wait results. The old people are dying. What reason do you *set forth* for agitating a more rapid emancipation?

I *know* that you are right *not to wait*. I *know* that I am right not to wait – but why? I do not know why. I cannot put it in words. I *must* know however and I feel sure you can make it plain to me. You think so *clearly*.

I took the liberty of sending your first letter – to some of the negro newspapers in America. It attracted a good deal of attention. They need to know more of the hopeful doings of their race so as to recognize *how much and how little* of their present degradation is due to caste prejudice and how much to their own personal inactivity[.]

Yours very truly
Cath. Impey

Letter 44
Allen to Nabuco

21 June 1883
New Broad Street

Dear Senhor Nabuco

I am directed by the Committee of this Society to tender you their sincere thanks for the trouble you have taken in forwarding to the Brazilian Govt. an address calling upon them to claim from the St. John del Rey Co. the back wages due to 220 slaves who died in bonds. They also would be glad if you will someday furnish them with a copy of the original document. Probably it will appear in print and a printed copy will suffice.

I hope you will kindly hold yourself free to attend an Anti-Slavery meeting at Dr. Inglebys private grounds near London on the 10th or 12th July. I will give you particulars later.

Yours very truly
Chas. H. Allen

Letter 45
Nabuco to Allen

27 July [1883]
20A Maddox Street, Regent Street

Dear Mr. Allen

The correspondence on Brazilian Slavery in *The Times* from Jundiahy[45] (I expect from Mr. Hammond, the same who has of late had a discussion on the subject with the *Rio News*, and is backing strongly and with personalities against us the Slavery interests), if not contested with the same ample space at the disposal of the writer, will be a blow to our cause, as it will be translated in Brazil and made to represent the British feeling of sympathies on the question.

I wish *The Times* would allow me space for an answer and a full statement of the series of reasons we Abolitionists have to pursue the course we have taken. My English being bad, although I can write better English than the nasty examples you have seen, I would accept with thanks any corrections from a competent person.

I am so busy that I would not like to write the answer unless sure of it being inserted, and I would feel very obliged to Mr. Sturge or Mr. Arthur Pease[46] if, bringing the subject before the Editor of *The Times* and telling him what influence to check the Abolitionist movement in Brazil articles of the kind of the one published to-day in the leading English journal are likely to have, they could obtain the insertion of my answer, and have the question treated in a leading article in a way favourable to our cause. This is really a very important question for us, as the effect of such a correspondence passing uncontradicted will be very great in Brazil where *The Times* seems the voice of civilization.[47]

---

45 *Slavery in Brazil* (from a correspondent at Jundiahy, São Paulo), *The Times*, 27 July 1883. The article argued, at enormous length, that 'the total abolition of slavery in Brazil cannot be accomplished without bringing with it most serious consequences to the financial prosperity of the country'. The immediate emancipation of over 1 million slaves would lead to 'ten years of darkness and ruin . . . an interregnum of anarchy, bloodshed and misery between the freeing and the perfect establishment of free labour'. The writer concluded: 'As a nation . . . Brazil is sick, and needs all the gentle care her friends can give her. That she will recover no one doubts . . . if she can but get help, moral and material, to beat down the monster anarchy which will clutch her by the throat if her emancipation of slavery be not very thoughtfully and prudently carried out'.

46 Arthur Pease 1837–98, MP Whitby 1880–5, committee member, future president of the society (1888–98).

47 No reply by Nabuco to this article was published in *The Times*.

Yours truly
J. Nabuco

Letter 46
Alexander to Nabuco

28 July 1883

Dear Senhor Nabuco

Enclosed I send you cuttings from *Cook's Excursionist*, which will give you the fares to Milan.[48] You will be able to estimate other expenses for yourself, as well as I can do.

I trust you will not, however, allow those expenses to be any hindrance to your going. We have a fund applicable to Anti-Slavery purposes, out of which the expenses of our journey to Berlin at the time of the Congress were paid and I am sure that I have only to mention the matter to Mr. Sturge, whom I expect to see at the Anti-Slavery Committee on Friday, I ensure you the repayment of your expenses. If you are good enough to do the work, I am sure we ought to find the money.

As to the other point I will communicate with Sir Travers Twiss and Dr. Stubbs, so as to make sure that your paper[49] shall have full consideration. At present we have no considerable number of subjects likely to lead to discussion, so that there can be no sufficient reason for your being excluded – indeed you may take my assurance that time will be found for you.

I much hope that you will be with us and shall look forward with great interest to the reading of your paper.

Yours very truly
Joseph G. Alexander

48 For the International Law Association annual meeting in Milan, September 1883.

49 The paper, a review of the slave trade and slavery, written and delivered in French, was published in the *Anti-Slavery Reporter*, October 1883.

Letter 47
Alexander to Nabuco

4 August 1883

Dear Senhor Nabuco

I am much obliged for your letter received this morning, and shall have much pleasure in proposing Senhor Alcoforado[50] and yourself as members of the International Law Association. I hope he will be able, as well as yourself, to be with us at Milan.

I am happy to tell you that at the Anti-Slavery Committee yesterday I met Mr. Sturge and the other gentlemen who are co-trustees with myself of the 'Friends' Anti-Slavery Fund, and I am authorized to offer you the sum of L 20 to pay your expenses to Milan.

With regard to your paper, I am sorry that I omitted before to write to you as to the best mode of presenting it. If you would not find it too much work, I think it would be very desirable that the paper should be presented *both in French and in English.* We shall have a large number of Italians and probably Swiss and others who would be able to read it much better in French – on the other hand, there are always a number of English and Americans who can't read French with comfort, and as the report is in English the paper would have to be translated if it is to appear there.

You will find it much cheaper and more satisfactory to get the French edition printed in Paris: if you send the Ms. by post to Messrs. Marchal Billard & Co. (see address on next page), the publishers of the Journal *du Droit International Privé,* they would do it very well, and would send you the proofs to correct. As for the English is concerned, I shall be most happy to revise it. I should say that 200 of each would be an amply sufficient number to have printed.

If Senhor Alcoforado would favour us with a paper on any subject of International Law, public or private, we should be very glad. It is doubtful whether we have another meeting of the Council before we go to Milan, and in that case you will not be elected members previously, but this is a mere matter of form.

Hoping to meet you in good time at Milan, I am
Yours very truly
Joseph G. Alexander
Marchal Billard & Co.
27 place Dauphiné, Paris
In London you could not do better than go to Mr. Kingdon who prints the *Anti-Slavery Reporter.*

50 Not identified.

Letter 48
Alexander to Nabuco

24 August 1883

Dear Senhor Nabuco

Perhaps under the circumstances mentioned in your letter it is not worth while any further to attempt a meeting, but you will find me here from 10:15 to 1 o'clock tomorrow if you should desire to call. I do not know that I have something important to say to you on the subject of your paper: you expressed a wish to come to an understanding with me about it but perhaps the answers I gave to your questions as to printing in French or English do sufficiently meet your wants. I have by me still a considerable number of copies of my paper, and I intend bringing them with me to Milan for distribution.

I received yesterday from Mr. Allen the enclosed cheque for you, which I have endorsed over to you accordingly. I have a Council meeting of the Association this afternoon at which I shall propose you and Senhor Alcoforado as members – also Mr. Allen, who is coming over to Milan from Switzerland.

Yours very truly
Joseph G. Alexander

Letter 49
Nabuco to Allen

31 March 1884
33 Davies Street, Berkeley Square

Dear Mr. Allen

I hope you are in good health after your short holiday. I am going to take mine now, as ever since I came from Milan my health has been very poor and I have lost 2 stones without knowing the cause of my extreme nervous debility.

I hope the long sea-voyage and change of climate and surroundings will prove successful if what I am suffering is simply over-work combined with home-sickness and want of my native sun.

I think of leaving for Brazil on the 15th and to stay away 4 months. But who knows? Meanwhile, I am glad to tell you, the Abolitionist movement there is getting every day stronger and I trust my holiday will be employed in agitating the question still more than it has yet been. The moment seems to me to have arrived for some energetic kind of action.

Your 'Gordon Pasha's Life' seems to be very popular.[51] What tremendous blunder his Proclamation was! Happily for us it came after the Milan Conference.

I will call on you some day next week and would feel obliged if you did kindly present to Mrs. Allen my respects and best wishes for her own and her children's welfare.

I remain always
Yours very sincerely
Joaq. Nabuco

---

51 Allen had recently published *Never to be Taken Alive: A Biography of General Gordon*, a prophetic title as it turned out. General Charles Gordon (1833–85) had been appointed governor-general of Sudan on the Upper Nile following the British occupation of Egypt in 1882. Faced with a revolt by fundamentalist Muslim forces the British government instructed him to organise the evacuation of Sudan. Gordon, however, chose to stay and defend 'civilisation' against 'barbarism', though to the consternation of the Anti-Slavery Society he issued a proclamation sanctioning slavery in Sudan in order to secure local support for his rule. When in March 1884 Khartoum came under siege from the Sudanese rebels Gordon was more or less abandoned by the British government until his fate became a popular cause. Khartoum was only finally relieved by British troops at the end of January 1885, two days after Gordon himself had been killed and beheaded (on 26 January 1885).

Letter 50
Allen to Nabuco (in Rio de Janeiro)

13 June 1884
55 New Broad Street

My dear Senhor

I trust you have long 'ere this arrived safely at your destination and are in better health. I was very sorry not to see you before you went. My journey to Morocco and subsequent illness prevented it.

Morocco is now occupying a prominent position and my visit was well timed. The article which I wrote for *The Times* which appeared in their columns 12 May and the Editorial thereon 14th brought the question forward and now the action of France is helping to raise the interest in that hitherto neglected country. You will see my article in this month's *Reporter*.

Egypt is still in the same muddle, if not worse. Out of it I hope we may see that the question of slavery is doomed to be settled once for all. It is time some limit should be fixed to the holding of slaves. I shall be glad to hear from you with any good news as to Emancipation in Brazil and that other provinces are following the noble example of Ceará.[52]

Poor Gordon! We are still in great fear for him – but I hope he may escape with his life and health. He must have had a terrible time in the weltering heat of the Soudan, in a besieged city [Khartoum].

We are very busy preparing for our great Jubilee Meeting of 1 August next and trying to raise a Jubilee fund, as we have only about £100 left and are nearly bankrupt. I wonder if any Abolitionists in Rio would like to subscribe to our jubilee fund. Mr. Sturge is very unwell and has not been in town for many weeks – but I hope he is now getting somewhat better. We are all well at home and all join in kind regards and best wishes.

Yours very sincerely
Chas. H. Allen

52 Slavery was abolished throughout the northern province of Ceará on 25 March 1884. Nabuco had announced this in a letter to *The Times* on 8 April 1884. Nabuco had earlier reported the genesis of the abolitionist movement in Ceará in the spontaneous refusal of the *jangadeiros*, the raftsmen of Fortaleza harbour, to carry slaves to steamers waiting to transport them to slave markets in the south, and the success of the Cearense Libertadora in freeing slaves in three districts of Ceará, in a letter to the *Anti-Slavery Reporter*, 5 April 1883 (published the same month). In a letter to *The Times*, 28 May 1883 (published 1 June), he had reported the news by telegraph of the abolition of slavery in the city of Fortaleza on 24 May. In July 1884 Amazonas became the second province to abolish slavery.

Letter 51
Nabuco to Allen

19 November 1884
Pernambuco,

Dear Mr. Allen

I am here in Pernambuco fighting for a place in Parliament. The election takes place on the 1st Dec. and by the 4th you will be able to know by writing to the Brazilian Legation if I was elected or not. You know we have an Abolitionist Administration now,[53] and I am strongly supported by it. I have made several speeches in public places and the election here is the one the Abolitionists are fighting more in earnest in the Empire. It will be a well won victory if we triumph in Pernambuco. I was never so busy in my life.

Be kind enough to remember me always and to present my respects to your associates of the 'Anti-Slavery'. Ever since I came from London I have been working steadily for our cause in Rio, S. Paulo and here. My election is very probable.

Yours very sincerely
J. Nabuco

53 The Liberal senator Manuel Pinto de Sousa Dantas (1831–94) had assumed the presidency of the council of ministers on 6 June 1884, with a programme that included various measures related to slavery, in particular the emancipation of slaves aged 60 and over without indemnification of the slave-owners. The abolitionists were enthusiastic and redoubled their efforts to mobilise pubic opinion. Nabuco wrote to Barão de Penedo, the Brazilian minister in London, on 23 June: 'We have taken an immense step forward; Dantas has given us much strength'. But the chamber, despite having a Liberal majority, failed to support Dantas in a vote of confidence on 28 July (52 votes in favour, 59 votes against). He therefore requested the dissolution of the chamber and called new elections for 1 December. On 8 September 1884 *The Times* published a long editorial, which was forwarded to the Brazilian government by Penedo, defending the Dantas bill and criticising the opponents of abolition.

Letter 52
Alexander to Nabuco

6 December 1884

My dear Senhor Nabuco

Mrs. Alexander and I were both very sorry to find that you had left England without our having had the pleasure of receiving you in Croydon. I trust, however, that it may not be very long before you again visit our island, and that we may then have the satisfaction of a visit from you. I hope your health has been restored by this time in the climate of your own beautiful country.

I write for the purpose, especially, of sending you a copy of the draft bill on slavery and the slave trade which I have been drawing for the Anti-Slavery Society. It carries out some of the suggestions you brought before us at Milan, and you will see that it also deals with the question of English companies holding slaves. Under its provision there can, if it passes, be no more cases that like of the St. John del Rey Co. suffered to pass by with impunity. I shall be glad of any suggestions you have to make on this bill. They will probably reach me before it has actually been presented to parliament.

We are hoping that the Berlin conference[54] will at last take some step to assimilate the slave trade with piracy in international law. You will have seen in the *Times* the report of one interview with Lord Granville,[55] and the *Anti-slavery Reporter* will furnish you with a fuller report from which you will find that the resolutions you carried at Milan with regard to slavery were not omitted to be brought to his Lordship's attention. We are very glad Sir Travers Twiss is at Berlin as legal adviser to our Embassy.

I was interested to hear at the Antislavery Committee yesterday of your candidature for the Brazilian Parliament and hope you will be this time elected. May God's blessing attend your efforts in the cause of the slave!

I am
Yours very truly
Joseph G. Alexander

54 The second congress of Berlin convened by Bismarck, November 1884–February 1885, at which the European great powers discussed the creation of areas of free trade in Africa, and especially in the Congo basin.

55 Lord Granville, Foreign Secretary.

Letter 53 (torn fragment – not all of it legible) Allen to Nabuco

8 [December 1884]
55 New Broad Street

My dear Senhor

I was much obliged for the copy of the *Tribuna* containing your eloquent speech to the Electors of Recife. I sent it to Mr. Crawford, who has read it and given me a short epitome for the *Reporter*. I also received your letter of 19th inst. [letter 51] which was read at our Committee on Friday last. Mr. Sturge and all those present desire to be very warmly remembered to you, and I need not say that you have our very warmest wishes for your election to the Brazilian Parliament. I am sure that the oppressed slaves can find no more able or eloquent . . . than yourself.

. . . to the Embassy to . . . have been elected, but . . . have no reply . . . by Book Post copy . . . speeches made at our Jubilee meetings which I think will interest you, and being in a bound form will be found more easy of reference. I also forward you Printers Proof of Draft Copy of Bill to amend the laws relating to the Slave Trade. Mr. Alexander has had the principal share in drawing up this Bill [letter 52] which now awaits the criticism of Mr. Bryce, M.P.[56] Meanwhile we shall be very glad to receive your suggestions as to any amendment that you may . . . requires . . . As our . . . has adjourned till the middle of February, there will probably be time to receive your reply.

With kind regards in which Mrs. Allen would join me were she here.
I am
Yours sincerely
Chas. H. Allen

56 James Bryce (1838–1922), historian, Liberal MP, briefly in 1885 under-secretary of state for foreign affairs, future British ambassador to Washington 1907–13.

Letter 54
Nabuco to Allen

22 February 1885
Rio de Janeiro

Dear Mr. Allen

I sent you some papers with news of my reception here. I claim to have been elected for the city of Pernambuco, but the Conservatives together with Pro Slavery Liberals are trying to turn me out of the House. It will give rise here to a decided movement against Parliament if they succeed. As I am a strong supporter of the Dantas Cabinet both to defeat him and to give a blow to the abolitionist cause our opponents are doing everything to annul my election, which was the first of its kind in Brazil quite an English or American election disputed in public meetings instead of the corrupt system of intimidating and buying votes in which Slavery puts its force. The public mind is very excited.

The unanimity of Abolitionist feeling in all large towns of Brazil is complete and we are making very rapidly the most peaceful emancipation the world ever saw in such large scale.

Do remember me to Mrs. Allen, whom I hope to see again in London, hoping to see you some day here where you could come in Anti-Slavery work and at the same time see the country.

Yours very truly
Joaquim Nabuco

I will send you this month a book I am printing with 12 or 13 of the 20 long speeches on Abolition which I delivered during my Recife (Pernambuco) campaign.[57] I was very ill when I went and the work cured me. My best regards to Mr. Sturge. J.N.

---

57 *Campanha abolicionista no Recife: eleições de 1884* (Rio de Janeiro: Leuzinger, 1885). Twelve speeches are included. The most famous meetings were those held in the Teatro Santa Isabel with audiences of over 4,000. The election (1 December 1884) was contested by Nabuco for the Liberals and Machado Portela for the Conservatives. Nabuco lost by a small margin, but because of disturbances, accusations of fraud and even some deaths the election was annulled. A second election was held on 9 January 1885. Claiming victory in the December election, the Conservatives abstained in January. Nabuco, therefore, won unopposed. The result, however, was later overturned in the chamber of deputies (see notes 58, 59 and 60).

Letter 55
Nabuco to Allen

17 May 1885
Rio de Janeiro

Dear Mr. Allen

After a long suspense my claim to represent the capital of Pernambuco, the city of Recife, was defeated in the House by a coalition of Conservatives and pro-slave liberals against the united forces of Liberals, Republicans and Abolitionists Conservatives.[58] The House has thus admitted to a seat a man whom the *majority* of the electorate had in a legal election repudiated. I send you a leading article of the newspaper *O Paiz* in which my exclusion from Parliament is severely discussed. In Recife the news produced a great shock as you will see by the *Rio News* and as a new election is to take place on the 7th June in one of the districts of the Province[59] the liberal candidates have withdrawn in my favour, so that I have again a chance, although a slight one – it being an agricultural district this time, of entering Parliament. The seven Liberal votes which added to the Conservative [which] rejected me were of men entirely dependent on the patronage of Slavery or of coffee-merchants here. The new Ministry[60] comes to power distrusting us and distrusted by us Abolitionists, while it has promise of support from Conservatives and pro-slavery Liberals. But it has already introduced the same bill nearly for which Senhor Dantas was

58 On 12 May the chamber of deputies, elected in December and meeting for the first time in March, had not recognised Nabuco's election in Recife on 9 January and, by 51 votes to 48, awarded the seat to Machado Portela for his election, subsequently annulled, on 1 December 1884 (see note 57).

59 The new election was held in the fifth district of Pernambuco, which comprised the *municípios* of Nazaré and Bom Jardim. The election was called on the death of deputy Antônio Epaminondas de Melo.

60 On 4 May the newly elected chamber had supported a vote of no confidence in the Dantas cabinet by 52 votes to 50. Dantas, defeated a second time, had no alternative but to resign. In his place the emperor called on another Liberal senator, José Antônio Saraiva, to form a government. He took office on 6 May. To overcome resistance to the Dantas bill in the chamber, Saraiva introduced an indemnification clause, which disappointed and angered the abolitionists. Under the bill, which soon after became law, slaves aged 60 and over were freed but were obliged to work three more years for their former masters, who at the same time received indemnification for the loss of their slaves. Slaves under 60 who were freed through an emancipation fund had to work another five years for their former owners. Nabuco criticised the changes to the bill in a pamphlet entitled *O erro do Imperador*.

overthrown, which shows the strength of the movement against Slavery. The Cabinet think their bill will put an end to Slavery by purchase in seven or eight years. We will fight the indemnity principle, but will end, I believe, by voting the funds, however unfair and unjust the principle of making us, and poor people, and the old slaves themselves, besides all those who have spontaneously liberated their slaves, pay taxes for the redemption of other people's slaves.

If I am elected on the 7th I will telegraph to the Brazilian Legation – so that you may know when you receive this what my fate has been.

I long to see myself again in London, but both by the article of the *O Paiz* and by such a behaviour as that of the Liberal candidates to give up their place in my interest you will see how difficult it is for me to leave my country.

Yours sincerely
Joaquim Nabuco

Letter 56
Allen to Nabuco

8 June 1885
55 New Broad Street

My dear Sir

I see that the Rio Mail leaves tomorrow, and with it goes my friend Mr. Lamoureux the Editor of the *Rio News*,[61] whose acquaintance I have had the great pleasure to make during his short visit to this City. That Gentleman gave me the sad news a few days since that your election to the Chamber of Deputies had been declared invalid by a majority of only three! This is another blow to the cause of Abolition in Brazil, but I trust it will only be temporary and that you will yet obtain the seat for which you are so eminently qualified. I sent the account of this disaster to *The Times*, in which it appeared on Friday 2nd inst.[62] Mr. Lamoureux has written me a valuable and interesting letter on the state of the law in Brazil as regards setting slaves free at the age of 60 years[63] and I regret to find that there is no such law in force; only a proposition by the late Minister [Dantas], which is probably about to be superseded by a proposal to extend the age to 65 *with compensation* to the slave owners! This is simply monstrous as now after working the poor wretches nearer to death, these men are to be paid for giving freedom to their worn out slaves with one foot already in the grave!

I hope the planters may be defeated though I fear they have it all their own way just now.

The day of retribution will however come, and probably sooner than they expect.

We are very busy just now with the Soudan question as you will probably see next mail, for we hope to hold a public meeting soon at the Mansion House to discuss this subject.

---

61 Andrew Jackson Lamoureux, a graduate of Cornell University, had gone to Brazil in 1877 where he became proprietor and editor of the *Rio News* (until 1901).

62 In fact Allen's letter was dated 4 June, published 5 June:

> Sir, I very much regret to learn that a telegram just received from Brazil states that the anti-slavery Deputy, Senhor Joaquim Nabuco, who claimed the contested seat for Pernambuco, has been rejected by the Chamber of Deputies by three votes . . . I regret also to learn that the new project for emancipation extends the age of the negro to be set free to 65 years instead of 60, thus prolonging the agony. I am, sir, yours faithfully, Charles H. Allen.

63 Letter not found.

The Government are inclined to leave the Soudan to relapse into barbarism, the slave dealers will have it all their own way for a while. This Egyptian business[64] has been a bad one, and we have done nothing but muddle it over since we went to the country. The desertion of Gordon for so many months until the country insisted upon a relief expedition being sent – which of course was *too late* – will form a black page in our history.

To me Gordon's death is a personal and quite irretrievable loss, as I knew him so intimately and he was so closely allied with our work.

I shall be glad to hear from you when you have time to write and meanwhile I beg to offer you the sincere condolences of all our Committee on your defeat – so disastrous to the best interests of Brazil.

Believe me
Yours very sincerely
Chas. H. Allen

64 See note 51.

Letter 57
Allen to Nabuco

22 June 1885
55 New Broad Street

My dear Sir

Your letter of 17th May [letter 55] was extremely interesting. I had already heard from M. Lamoureux of your rejection by the Chamber owing to a pro slavery combination. A short time afterwards I was delighted to hear from Senhor Rodriguez[65] that you had been elected by another constituency and this notice I inserted in *The Times*.[66]

Shortly afterwards, 19th inst., a leader appeared in which my first letter was referred to.[67] This contained an account of your rejection: a copy of that issue

65 José Carlos Rodrigues (1844–1923), Brazilian journalist, who had lived in the United States, where he published the newspaper *O Novo Mundo* (1870–9), before moving to London in 1882. In 1890, with a number of associates, he bought the *Jornal do Comércio* from the conde de Villeneuve for eight million francs (3,200 *contos de réis*) and edited it for 25 years.

66 Letter dated 11 June, published 12 June:

> Sir
>
> . . . The election of this well-known Abolitionist deputy so soon after his rejection by an organised opposition of slaveholders in the Chamber has a very important bearing upon the agitation now going on throughout Brazil in favour of emancipation. The institution of slavery dies hard, and we shall probably yet see some severe struggles before it receives its final deathblow in Brazil. Publicity given to the movement in the columns of The Times always does much to assist the efforts of the Abolitionists, the planters being peculiarly sensitive to the criticism of the English people. I am, Sir, yours faithfully, Charles H. Allen

67 *The Times* editorial of 19 June welcomed the fact that the Saraiva government was following in the steps of its predecessor, in making 'a comprehensive attempt for the declared purpose of getting rid of slavery in Brazil'. But the defeat of Dantas's bill for the emancipation of slaves over 60 in the chamber of deputies and the result of the election that followed was proof that 'the country is not in favour of abolition, as the term is understood in Brazil, but that it prefers some measure less entirely at variance with the slaveholders' interests'. The bill for the gradual extinction of slavery in Brazil by freeing slaves over 65 with indemnification for their owners introduced by the Saraiva government [and explained in detail in a letter from A. de Souza Corrêa, Secretary, Brazilian Legation, London published at the same time] 'will be closely scrutinised both there and in this country'. Theoretically, even if the bill passed (and it was sure to be contested by the slave owning interest) slavery need not end until 1935 when the youngest slave in Brazil (aged 15) reached 65. But by also increasing,

of *The Times* is forwarded you by this Mail, also *Times* for today containing extract of your letter to me.[68] The Abolitionists in Brazil will see that they have the support of the British public, and of this Society in their endeavour to oppose the nefarious system of buying the old worn out slaves from the planters by money raised from the general public. Surely when slaves have worked up to the age of 65 they have earned their freedom without calling upon the national purse. It would be much more just to compel the planters to maintain their worn out slaves for the rest of their lives. We congratulate you heartily on your election, and feel sure that you will lead the crusade against this unjust Bill with your usual eloquence and vigour.

Wishing you all success
I am
Yours sincerely
Chas. H. Allen

---

through new taxes and loans, the emancipation fund by which slave-owners freeing slaves were indemnified, the government, Souza Corrêa argued, hoped to end slavery by 1892. *The Times* remained sceptical, however. Moreover, even when there were no more slaves in Brazil 'there will be plenty of persons whom a Louisiana planter would have described as held in involuntary service'. But, *The Times* concluded:

> it is useless to complain that a defeat of the abolitionist party is not followed by a bill which an abolitionist could approve, or that the Parliamentary triumph of the slaveholders does not promise the extinction of slavery in reality as well as in name. The title of the bill is fair-sounding enough, but it will mislead nobody who will be at the pains of reading the contents.

68 Allen letter dated 19 June, published 22 June:

> Sir, In confirmation of the views so ably stated in the editorial columns of The Times of this day as to the hollow nature of the proposed scheme for purchasing the freedom of slaves in Brazil, I shall be glad if you will allow me to publish a few lines from a letter [from Nabuco] lately received by me [letter 55] . . . His [Nabuco's] views are identical with those contained in your editorial, and are of special value, coming as they do from an experienced Abolitionist. I am, Sir, yours faithfully, Charles H. Allen

Letter 58
Nabuco to Allen

23 June [1885]
Pernambuco

Dear Mr. Allen

I send you cuttings of the newspapers here and in Rio about my election and the reception I had here. Never was such a scene seen before. More than 50,000 people took part in it and it was a general holiday, all the city being in flags, music, flowers and illuminations in the evening. This shows the strength the abolitionist movement has acquired, it is a national resurrection or still better a national birth.

Yours devotedly,
J. Nabuco

Letter 59
Nabuco to Allen

6 August 1885
Rio de Janeiro

Dear Mr. Allen

I have to thank you for your communication to *The Times*. We have formed in the Chamber of Deputies a Parliamentary Abolitionist Group, the Statutes of which I enclose. Until the end of this Legislature the fight over Slavery will be a hard one. The Government are carrying their bill through.[69] The two old parties both formed chiefly of slave-holders and representatives of the political power of Slavery are supporting the Cabinet of Senhor Saraiva in fear of a more advanced one and voting his bill to avoid the introduction of a really honest and straightforward measure. We of course are opposing that shameful Act through which Slavery will be perpetuated in the National Debt, threatening the nation with bankruptcy. I said the other day in the House that it had converted itself into a Marrocos Slave Market. They voted a tablet of prices for slaves fixing the price of £90 for the slaves under 30 years of ages, £80 for slaves between 30 and 40 years, £60 for slaves between 40 and 50, £40 for slaves between 50 and 55 and £20 for slaves from 55 to 60. Slaves of 60, 61, 62 years will be nominally free bound to work three years still for their masters, slaves of 63 bound to work two years, slaves of 64 bound for one year and slaves of 65 upwards actually freed. The prices above are scandalous, and the scandal is greater because the bill alters the present law which enables a slave to redeem himself through his acquired *peculium* subject to arbitration. By the new bill the evaluation is abolished and the slave will have to pay for his freedom the whole of the price fixed for slaves of his age, without any regard to his personal

---

69 With the introduction of modifications to the Dantas bill (see letter 55) Saraiva secured the support of the Conservative minority in the chamber and the bill was approved on 13 August. But, lacking confidence in his ability to deliver the same result in the senate, dominated by the Conservatives, Saraiva then resigned. After various Liberals refused to form a government, the emperor invited senator João Maurício Wanderley, barão de Cotegipe (1815–89), the leader of the Conservatives, to become president of the council of ministers, after he had guaranteed that the bill would be approved in the senate. Cotegipe took office on 20 August and immediately fulfilled his promise. The Saraiva-Cotegipe law, more popularly known as the law of sexagenarians, became law on 28 September 1885. In the meantime, the Liberals had carried a vote of no confidence in the new government (by 63 votes to 49 on 24 August) and on 26 October Cotegipe requested the dissolution of the chamber, with elections to be held on 15 January 1886.

conditions. But what makes those prices scandalous is that they amount to the double and in many provinces to three times more, of the current prices. So that the Government raise so very high the value of the slaves that it will be impossible for any province to do hereafter what Ceará and Amazonas did. I mean to free themselves through the falling off in slave's values as the slaves have now a price which will prevent people from giving them up and will make every slave master wait for his turn to have his slaves bought off by the State at a higher rate than he could get in the market. The Government have thus found means to make the slave market recover, to restore their old life to transactions over slaves and to insure slave property at the expense of the taxpayers, abolitionists, non slave-holders, foreigners, poor people, people who already liberated their own slaves and lastly and most shameful freedmen and slaves.

It is altogether an attempt of Slavery, condemned as it was by the national voice, to save itself from utter failure at the sacrifice of national ruin.

The political oligarchy which govern this country could not resist the cry for abolition, but they contrived to replace the abolition bill by one for the liquidation of slavery on the best possible terms for persons interested in it. After having raised the price of slave property they introduced as the two abolition factors in their scheme – 1st. a depreciation of value of so much a year, starting from 2% and ending by 12%, combined to leave the slave at the end of thirteen years without a value and therefore free, and 2nd additional tax of 5% on the whole of the national taxation (exports only excluded to spare the slave-owner alone) to be divided in three equal parts. With one the Government will buy slaves below 60 years of age to free them at once; with another the Government will pay the interests of a 5% issue of bonds to buy off for half their declared value the whole of the slaves employed in plantations whose owners will agree to receive half their value and five years of apprenticeship to declare them free and only employ free labour in their estates; with the third part of the Government will subsidize colonization for the agricultural establishments now cultivated by the slaves. It is altogether a futile and absurd scheme for helping the planters to get rid of their slaves at a *minimum* of loss, a scheme which will impose great sacrifices to the taxpayers without insuring any actual good to the agricultural industries of the country. But planters accept it as the best thing they could get and hoping in their renewed contract with the State to hold slaves for thirteen years longer to pay off their slave debt at the cost of the slave labour. The bill provides only for the *nominal* slaves, as the *ingenuous* [sic, ingênuos], who are slaves too, being bound up to serve the masters of their mother until they are 21 years old (and therefore as slaves the real slaves as nobody is to be a slave in Brazil for more than 21 years, thank God, the nation would not allow it) are altogether forgotten and left outside the beneficent sphere of this heavenly born Abolition Act.

The Act besides imposes a fine of £100 on those who will help a slave to run away – an outrageous measure as slaves who run away often run away from fear of dying under the lash and no man of honour could avoid helping the poor wretch; and states than no runaway slave can be freed, which means that to recover his freedom he must first go back to the lash or to what is death to him.

I have said enough to justify our opposition to a bill which has no other aim but to delude the world and the country, which is very popular among slave-holders and their creditors, but which will be ruinous to the country and to the poor people, called upon to save from utter bankruptcy the mortgaged long ago and exhausted Slavery of this county. We are going to increase our debt and our taxation when the budget has a large *deficit*, which each year bequeaths to its follower, and when our currency is depreciated of 40%, a state of discredit to which our finance Ministers got so accustomed that they consider mere and ridiculous declamation anything said on that point. Slavery led us to ruin in every way. Its exclusive, intolerant, shut up spirit was for a long time the basis of a policy internally favourable in every point to backwardness and routine and externally to prestige and war. After the Paraguayan War[70] it changed its views and begun to press for material improvements, crying for railroads and the rest. The country on account of its immense coffee crop was said to be the richest in the world and the future was taxed with successive loans without any sense of what, in a vast and young country, exposed to all sorts of unforeseen expenditure, like the Ceará drought for instance, and eager to imitate every European Progress and possess each new material, moral, intellectual or social improvements of civilization, ought to be the proportions between the vital and the dead parts of the national budget. Now the harm is done. Our debt and war budget have grown tremendously and the weight is still to be increased as long as the winding up of slavery lasts.

Either in national finances or in agricultural prosperity; towards the soil it found; and finds virgin as it spreads, as well as towards the people it employs; with regard to our institutions from the throne to the electorate, in everything Slavery means failure and decomposition, weakness and atrophy. Only a new spirit totally opposed in agriculture and trade, in politics and education; can undo in centuries of freedom and justice the harm done in centuries of oppression and rapine. And unfortunately the Government believe without it we are lost. No wonder we Liberals do not follow blindly the Cabinet in this attempt to make the death of Slavery and its burying so soft that no one be aware of it – neither the master nor the slave, the country nor the world.

70 The Paraguayan war or the war of the Triple Alliance (Brazil, Argentina and Uruguay) against Paraguay, 1864–70.

Good bye – dear Mr. Allen, I have long enough occupied your attention.

Yours very truly
Joaquim Nabuco

Letter 60
Allen to Nabuco

14 August 1885
55 New Broad Street

Dear Senhor Nabuco

As you may well imagine we have all followed with great interest the important news from Brazil respecting your election to the Chamber of Deputies. Our sympathies are with you in every way and I now have the pleasure to forward you Copy of a Resolution passed at the last meeting of our Committee [7 August]. I hope you will be able successfully to resist the proposed loan for buying up worn out slaves. This is a monstrous proposition intended to put money into the pockets of the slave holders, at the expense of the nation and ought to be resisted to the last. In our next *Reporter*, I hope we shall be able to publish a few facts taken from the *Rio News*, respecting your triumphant return. The present number is so taken up with the accounts of our late meetings that we had no room for anything else. Perhaps before our next appearance in October I shall have the pleasure of hearing from you again. Meanwhile I thank you very much for the illustrated newspapers and for the pocket handkerchief containing so good a likeness of yourself, which is now hanging in the office.

Mr. Sturge continues in good health and is as full of antislavery energy as every.

Our Parliament has just risen and there will not be very much for us to do publicly at present. The elections in November will be an exciting time and I should think would result in a Liberal majority[71] notwithstanding Lord Randolph Churchill's confident predictions to the contrary.[72]

Believe me
Yours very sincerely
Chas. H. Allen
Mrs Allen joins me in kind regards and hearty congratulations.

---

71 The Liberal prime minister William Ewart Gladstone had resigned in July (in part because of his perceived mishandling of the Sudan question and the death of Gordon in Khartoum – see note 51). The Liberals did indeed win the election in November 1885 but because of gains by the Irish Nationalists they failed to secure an overall majority. Gladstone's third administration (1886) lasted only a few months.

72 Lord Randolph Churchill (1849–95), the third son of the seventh Duke of Marlborough and father of Winston Churchill, progressive Conservative MP. He served as chancellor of the exchequer (1886–92).

Enclosure:
Committee of Anti-Slavery Society *resolved*:
That this Committee has learned that with sincere pleasure and satisfaction of the triumphant return of *Senhor Joaquim Nabuco* as a Member of the Brazilian Parliament, and hereby offers to him its hearty congratulation after obtaining after so much labour against an organized opposition, a victory which cannot fail to advance the cause of freedom in Brazil, and to revive the drooping spirits of those staunch Abolitionists who have so long fought against the overwhelming forces of a Planter's coalition.

Letter 61
Allen to Nabuco

6 October 1885
55 New Broad Street

My dear Senhor

Your interesting letter of 6th August [letter 58] came duly to hand and you will see by the enclosed cutting from *The Times* of 2nd inst. that I have made use of it to answer the letter of Dr. E.F. França which appeared in *The Times* of 21st Sept.[73] That letter was full of fallacies. You did not mark your letters 'private and confidential', and my sending them to *The Times* was approved by you in your last. You certainly do not approve the Bill of Indemnification, nor do we. This Society did not at all approve of the vote of Twenty Millions given to the West Indian planters. Mr. Buxton accepted it at the last moment to get an Abolition Bill passed, but it was not his original motion. He wanted a *loan* of 10 Millions to the planters, but the House was suddenly surprised by the Minister into carrying a *gift* of 20 millions, and the Abolitionists had to make the best of it.

This Society has always regarded it as a mistake for the money mostly went to pay off mortgages on encumbered estates and this put money into the pockets

73 The letter of Ernesto Ferreira França, lawyer to the council of state, dated 22 August, was published on 21 September. In defending the Saraiva bill, which had been approved in the chamber on 13 August, França argued that 'the judicious and far-seeing statesman' Nabuco had himself never proposed any plan of immediate abolition and had never made liberation without indemnity part of his programme. The Dantas and Saraiva emancipation bills were similar except as regards the principle of indemnification: 'the cabinet of Senhor Dantas conceded indemnification as a favour, and that of Senhor Saraiva as a right'. 'By the end of the present year', França predicted, 'all the slaves of Brazil will be converted into servants, an interim civil condition that of itself will cease to exist within a few years, even before the end of the century'. He added; 'Indemnification, in the present instance, is not a payment for a property, but a compensation for rights acquired and which were bound up in the economic system of the country, in which all are interested'. In his answer to França dated 30 September, published 2 October, to which he attached Nabuco's letter of 6 August, Allen insisted that Nabuco distinctly repudiated all approval of the Indemnification Bill: 'his disapproval of taxing the whole country to buy the slaves from the planters could scarcely be more strongly expressed'. And in this Nabuco had the full support of the Anti-Slavery Society which had never adopted the principle that indemnification was a right. Nabuco's letter of 6 August and Allen's of 30 September were reprinted in the *Anti-Slavery Reporter* October 1885, with commentary.

of those who had advanced to needy planters.

Dr. França would appear from his letter to know more about what the annals of the Society show than we do ourselves! I hope you will approve of my sending your last letter to *The Times*. I shall always consider I may publish anything you are good enough to send me unless it is marked 'Private'.

Please let us know exactly how the matter now stands, as the telegrams are confusing. Is the Bill now actual law? It would seem that you are to have a fresh election, therefore I imagine the Indemnification Bill may have fallen through at the last. You have our best wishes for your re-election on an Abolitionist platform. Mrs. Allen joins me in kind regards to yourself. We are in the throes of house-moving having migrated from Highgate to 13 Well Walk – Hampstead N.W. where we hope to welcome you some day. Will all best wishes believe me

Yours sincerely and truly
Chas. H. Allen

Letter 62 (fragment only)
Allen to Nabuco

[January 1886]

. . . As the mail leaves tomorrow I take the opportunity of heartily wishing you a happy new year on behalf of the Committee and myself, to which Mr. Teall[74] desires to add his best wishes.

We have been rather at a loss to understand the exact position of the antislavery question in Brazil, not having had the pleasure of hearing from you for some months. As far as we can understand it we fear that the Saraiva Bill has become law,[75] and that the whole nation is to be taxed to buy up the slaves from the planters at very exorbitant prices. We believe also that Parliament has been dissolved, and that probably you are at this moment in the throes of electioneering business. If so you have your best wishes for your success.

Before this reaches you I trust we may receive one of your interesting and valuable letters.

I have just returned from a visit to Morocco where in company with Mr. Crawford, ex Consul in Cuba, and one of our Committee I have been spending 5 or six weeks making inquiries as to the slave trade in that country and the various acts of oppression to which the people are constantly subjected. As we shall publish the information we have received I need not repeat it here. When Parliament meets we hope to be able to get some public notice of the condition of Morocco.

I am glad to inform you that our valued Chairman, Mr. Sturge, appears to be in remarkably good health, which we trust may long continue.

With kind regards in which Mrs. Allen cordially unites
I am,
Yours very truly
Chas. H. Allen

---

74 J. Estoe Teall, Charles Allen's assistant for 20 years from 1877 until his death aged 41, in 1897.

75 See letter 59.

Letter 63
Nabuco to Allen

23 January 1886
Pernambuco

Dear Mr. Allen

The election took place on the 15th. inst. and I was defeated in this city. The majority of the Conservative candidate over me is wholly due to the pressure of the Government on the public *employees*, who form a large portion of the small electorate of this town, and to the promises of employment profusely distributed among the poor classes of our people. (While the large slave-owners made every dependent of them vote as one man against me the negroes, who are numerous, were not all faithful to our cause and voted largely for the slavery flag. I went to more than one black elector and asked for his vote – I cannot, Sir, I promised to vote with the Conservatives. I am engaged – Engaged! That poor man did not know in his ignorance of social solidarity that he was engaged to vote for me two centuries ago when his ancestors were brought here enslaved from Africa and that his own colour ridiculed his 'previous engagement' excuse!

Brazil being so extensively a composite nation nobody more than I am glad to see that there is no possible way to trace here the colour line as a political boundary, so distinct as it is in the United States. Even the slavery question did not create a race feeling, altogether absent from our whole history and thence from our present national constitution. But at the same time this unconcern of the negroes in Brazil in the question of abolition, this way as soon as they cease to be slaves and jump at once to the dignity of citizens and electors of throwing off any blood tie whatever with their own enslaved race, is a sign more of how deeply the humiliation of slavery penetrated the mind and heart of the slave people and of the difficulty of the abolitionist movement had to fight against in Brazil. Here, in fact, instead of a solid negro vote, as in North America for the party that rose the cry of abolition, as a debt of gratitude of a whole race towards their liberators, we could see the negroes with worthy exceptions; following the party banner of their old masters as a remnant of the slave soul still alive in them.

Now that I have said this about my election let me give you an idea of the political situation in Brazil and its future prospects. The Conservatives have elected an almost unanimous Parliament. The very few Liberals who could break that actual unanimity are in their majority men who helped the Conservatives to power and whom they in turn treated as auxiliaries and very useful ones. Those disguised Conservatives in contrast with the true Liberals will give a semblance of division to the party in Parliament.

But the new Conservative victory is a sad news to Brazil. We during more than forty years had no real elections. The Emperor had only to call to power to chief of a party or section of party and that new minister would at once have a Chamber of Deputies of his own. In Portugal, in Spain, in Italy, and throughout Latin America, in different scale, though, this is still the existing electoral system. Parliament is an extension of the Government of the day. Lately we had a change in Brazil. The Liberal party reformed our old system of indirect election into the direct system and its principal statesman Senhor Saraiva pledged himself as prime-minister to have really free elections in the country. In fact the two first elections under the new Reform Act[76] were perfectly free, the opposition being more protected than the party in power; electing one time a large number of deputies and another defeating the government. Although a free grant, and freedom as the great German poet said, is only worthy when it is a conquest, the country was proud of its new independence in voting down the government in power and that feeling if it were encouraged could produce a sort of real self-reliance in the people and enable it to rule itself. Now the dream is over, the Conservatives could not resist the temptation, Senhor Cotegipe is not made of the same disinterested stuff as Senhor Saraiva, and we go back to the old system of each Government electing their own Parliament, fit to carry on their policy, that is to maintain them in power as long as it pleases the Emperor.

The short life of electoral freedom in Brazil and the spirit of political revenge now running wild through the country in the heart of both parties are facts which place us before very serious contingencies. The future is dark indeed. The discredit of the direct election means the fall of the last barrier between the dynasty and the republic. Wishing for earnest reforms which they have now no means to obtain from the electors, the Liberals are being strongly led in two different directions: the ones feel it is useless to fight against the present order of things and still more useless to hope in the existing institutions, while the others have faith in meeting mid-way the Republicans and in the end of the present reign preparing for its succession the advent of a new social form.

A feeling is very strong among the Abolitionists that the Emperor encouraged our movement to the point of forming an abolitionist government and then gave away to a pro-slavery coalition and allowed the slave-owners so to say to pocket in the national aspiration by converting their slaves in state debt for three to six times over their actual value. The late change of parties, due exclusively to his

76 The Lei Saraiva, 9 January 1881, had introduced the direct vote in legislative elections. With the intention of reducing the influence of government in elections, it also abolished voting by illiterates, except for those who had already registered to vote. Saraiva, president of the council of ministers, maintained a position of neutrality in the first elections for the chamber of deputies held under the new law, facilitating greater representation of the opposition.

own inspiration, brought about in the country a reaction against the liberating movement, the Conservative government was freely allowed by him to form an unanimous Chamber using all means of corrupting and intimidating the voters, pledging our future budget to the voracious hunger of a rising party of place-seekers, and in the midst of all this confusion the poor slave was made to pay for the movement started in his favour without even his consent. This feeling is now stranging very fast from the monarchy the sympathy and the good will of all earnest Abolitionists and, of course, the Republic is the gainer by what I call the error and I hope history in possession of all facts and documents will not call the crime of the Emperor. To superficial observers the Conservative victory may appear final and conclusive, but if they go deep in the causes of it they will see that it resulted entirely from the rottenness of slavery and from its deadly effect on the national character, and as both the throne and the institutions are raised on the Slavery foundation exclusively the future of the whole fabric is a matter of serious doubt and concern for those who like myself always thought that the way for the monarchy to root itself firmly in the heart of the nation was to put itself at the head of the liberation of this country from the treble slavery monopoly – of land, of labour, of capital, even if the Emperor who knows that his will is the only real power in Brazil and that he is practically as powerful under our parliamentary form of government as Augustus was under the forms of the Consular Republic – were to assume the rôle of a civilizing despot instead of ruling without any heartrending for more than forty five years over a large slave market and a nation's paralytic bed.

Believe me always, dear Mr. Allen,
Sincerely yours
Joaquim Nabuco

P.S. We formed yesterday here a liberal political association called Abolitionist and Federal Union of Pernambuco, with four hundred members to begin, all electors of this city. We mean to carry on our agitation although the glacial cold of the high regions has frozen some former enthusiasms of so-called abolitionists the strength of the abolitionist movement can be revived and we hope to make a dead letter of the new Act for purchase of slaves by the State above their price and for renewing the Slavery legal for another fourteen years. J.N.

I leave tomorrow for Rio.

Letter 64
Allen to Nabuco

16 April 1886
55 New Broad Street

My dear Senhor

Our last letters appear to have crossed; but you would see from a copy of *The Times* which I forwarded you, that I was able to publish a considerable portion of your valuable letter of the 23rd January [letter 63] in *The Times* of 18th February.[77] Since that date I have not had the pleasure of hearing from you, but we have received through the Under Secretary of State for Foreign Affairs [James Bryce – see letter 53], a copy of the Saraiva Act, respecting which we had a question asked in the House of Commons [by Sir J.W. Pease, 8 March]. That Act, so far as we can understand it, does not appear to be at all favourable to the slaves – indeed Mr. Bryce said that it was less liberal than the Government had hoped it would be.

We are every anxious to obtain a copy of the Regulations for carrying out the Act, as without that the Act is comparatively unintelligible. Would it be possible for you to assist us in obtaining a copy? Also, the Committee will be extremely obliged if you would kindly forward them one.

Naturally, we were all very much disappointed to find that you were unsuccessful in your last contest. The blow that the Antislavery cause has received at the last Brazilian election is a very serious one. *We* had a great disappointment also in the rejection of our good President Mr. Arthur Pease by the enlarged constituency.

Owing to the Irish business[78] our Parliament appears to be at present unapproachable for any other work, and we naturally have to keep quiet.

By this post I forward you copy of our Morocco Pamphlet, which I hope may interest you.

With kind regards in which we all join, not omitting Mrs. Allen and Mr. Teall.

I am, yours sincerely
Chas. H. Allen

77 Allen's letter dated 15 February. An edited version of Nabuco's letter of 23 January was also published in the *Anti-Slavery Reporter* March–April 1886.

78 The Irish question was one of the dominant issues in British politics in the late nineteenth and early twentieth centuries. Gladstone's short-lived third Liberal government of February–August 1886, dependent on the support of the Irish Nationalists, introduced the first of four Home Rule bills. It divided the Liberal Party and was defeated in the House of Commons. The Conservatives won the elections called in July with the support of the Liberal Unionists opposed to home rule for Ireland. See notes 71 and 72.

Letter 65
Nabuco to Allen, Private

18 April 1886
Rio de Janeiro

Dear Mr. Allen

I send you the enclosed letter for you to be kind enough to have it sent to *The Times,* and, if not accepted, to some other paper.

I am now writing a series of pamphlets,[79] of which I sent you already the first four. My friends are striving to raise the capital for a daily paper. I do not know if they will succeed. In case I despair of starting it, I may be forced to go back to England, to get my living there, as when the slave-owners, by *boycotting me*, reduced me to do in 1881. But at this moment, I am conscious that my leaving Brazil would be detrimental to the Liberal cause, not the Abolitionist only, and I will do the utmost to remain. Unfortunately the way to solve my individual problem together with the social problem is a very difficult one. If I were to start a paper I will ask you to be kind enough to send me occasionally some information.

Pray present my respects to Mrs. Allen and believe me
Yours very truly
Joaquim Nabuco

To the Editor of *The Times*[80]

Sir
I hope you will allow me some space in your columns to refer to two points on a recent article on W.L. Garrison,[81] by Mr. Goldwin Smith,[82] in *Macmillan's Magazine* [March 1886]. I would not so appeal to your kindness if those two points, besides their value with regard to the Abolitionist movement in the

79 Three pamphlets were published: *O erro do Imperador*, *O eclipse do abolicionismo*, and *Eleições liberais e eleições conservadoras*, all in 1886, by Leuzinger, Rio de Janeiro.

80 The letter was never published in *The Times*. It was later published in the *Anti-Slavery Reporter* August/September 1886.

81 William Lloyd Garrison (1805–79), editor of the *Boston Liberator* 1831–65, founder of the American Anti-Slavery Society in 1833.

82 Goldwin Smith (1823–1910), British-Canadian historian (Professor of Modern History, Oxford 1858–66, then Cornell), moved to Canada in 1871.

United States, did not concern the freedom of one million of living slaves in Brazil and the patriotism of the whole Party that fights for their freedom. Unfortunately, the Slavery question is not dead throughout the World, and as history repeats itself with the minutest fidelity in relation to it, the enemies of that institution having had and still having to fight everywhere against the same spirit, the same theories, and the same prejudices, practically result in strengthening the hands of the slave-owners in the present, chiefly when the blame comes from a man like Mr. Goldwin Smith, than whom nobody was ever more eloquent or indignant in denouncing slavery.

The two points in his article I find injurious to our work here are, the first, when he admits the right of slave-owners to compensation as any other holders of property; and the second, where he criticizes the Massachusetts Abolitionists for trying to raise public opinion in England. Now, as to the first, if compensation is a perfect right for the slave-owner, the State has no *right* to abolish Slavery unless it is prepared to pay the price of the slaves. If by abolishing Slavery without compensation, it violates the Ten Commandments, it has no right to abolish it. But suppose the State forms the conviction that Slavery is a crime. What side then to choose? Take a poor country like Brazil, which Slavery has ruined in her prospects, debased in her Government, humiliated in her people, devastated in her lands and crushed under a tremendous debt, that can only be paid by renewed loans. If we convince ourselves that slavery is a moral guilt and a national shame as well, and find ourselves at the same time unable to pay for its extinction without ruining our credit, robbing our creditors, and what is perhaps still worse, taxing to death the slave people themselves in order to save their masters, does Mr. Goldwin Smith mean to say that the Ten Commandments oblige us to go on lending our strong arm, our unwilling army, our magistrates and our Parliament, to hold on the slave market, to hunt up the run-away slaves, and to protect with our flag an institution we would consider nothing else but organized robbery, debauchery and assassination? I do not believe, Sir, that a nation is morally bound to ruin herself to acquire the right of stopping the practice of a crime, only because in her ignorance and servility to the dominant caste, she did not prevent it from carrying on that crime, as a trade. I leave aside all the points connected with the legality of slavery either in the United States, Spain or Brazil, as it would be only too easy to show that slavery, besides being a moral guilt, was everywhere a human blood smuggling. I simply ask – if any nation that allowed during a certain time an oppression to go on under the name of social institution, is morally held to pay with her whole ruin for its extinction, leaving, if she is unwilling to make the sacrifices, the victims of that oppression indefinitely in the hands of her would-be creditors until she can pay them her debt?

As to the second point, history well justified the Abolitionists in appealing to England. Did not Mr. Goldwin Smith himself take part in the powerful agitation, that the English Liberals, under the leadership of Mr. Cobden and Mr. Bright,[83] found necessary to raise in England to counteract the sympathy of some classes of your community with American Slavery? Did he not write a book full of the sparkles of his mind, to make England a moral ally of the Union? The American Abolitionists seem to have understood what a strong element in the battles of Slavery the English sympathies would necessarily be, and perhaps either if they had not, in time, looked for sympathizers among the leading forces of England, or if they had succeeded in conquering them all, many things might have been different for the worse, or the better, in the course of their great cause. But leaving North-America aside, is it not true that the political life of any country is a constant contribution to her own individuality of the mental and moral activity of the world, that ideas go round the Planet and civilization rises everywhere to the same level? To kill the spirit that keeps alive, say in Brazil, an institution like Slavery, dead in those countries whose progress, culture, enthusiasms and ideas do influence our social growth, as which are, so to say, the intellectual High Lands whose waters run down to us, we must bring as much as possible that doomed institution under the influence of foreign progress so as to contrast moral death within moral life abroad. As no greater service could ever have been done to the American Union than that which W.L. Garrison attempted to render to his country – of raising in England an unanimous sympathy with the work of the Abolitionists, so we, Brazilian Abolitionists, consider that no greater service could be done to Brazil than to have all the world condemning Slavery as piracy, since such a decree of the International Law would be echoed by her, to her own ransom and to her own freedom much sooner than our voice.

I might point out, too, that foreigners of all countries hold slaves here and by thus sharing the profits and the fate of slavery, they give it in the mind of our people, the sanction of their respective nationalities. The American Abolitionists were not mad to wish for foreign intervention of any kind, they only wished to cut the direct and indirect foreign feeders which swelled the slave interest and prestige, and, instead, to draw to their own side the moral influences abroad which have power on American ideas and warm or render active the national feelings. If this is want of patriotism as Mr. Goldwin Smith implies, then patriotism as such a narrow, backward and jealous feeling, has to be greatly improved before it becomes a tie of good will, freedom and justice to the different nations of the world.

I hope, Sir, you will excuse the length of this reply, written with all the respect I always felt for such a teacher of political morals as Mr. Goldwin Smith. But it was painful to me to have the two chief accusations made here

83 Richard Cobden (1804–65) and John Bright (1811–89), radical liberals.

against us – 1st that we are Communists, because we do not recognize the right of the slave-owner to compensation and say that slavery is simply an unjustifiable oppression for the sale of individual profit to which the State is not held to give any support, but on the contrary is bound to stop at once, and secondly, that we are no friends of our country because we ask for the sympathy of the world – thrust at us by the eloquent writer in whose pages we saw slavery denounced as the basest and the greatest crime of history. As for want of patriotism, let me add one last remark – which is the less patriotic: to denounce the crimes of slavery to the world as the best means of putting the ruling classes and the governing institutions on their trial and making them ashamed of the oppression in which they are accomplices, or in allowing foreigners to hold as their property, to flog and to debase, men who will be tomorrow, by virtue of the law, Brazilian citizens, Brazilian voters, and Brazilian soldiers?

I am, Sir,
Very obediently yours,
Joaquim Nabuco
Rio, 18 April 1886

Letter 66
Allen to Nabuco

21 May 1886
55 New Broad Street

My dear Senhor Nabuco

Your interesting letter addressed to the Editor of *The Times* arrived in due course, together with your letter to me of the 18th April [letter 65]. I quite agree with your remarks upon Professor Goldwin Smith's paper – indeed his paper does not appear to contain many merits. With regard to the compensation of slave owners for their ill-gotten property I presume you have not forgotten the eloquent words of the late Lord Brougham[84] which we have more than once pointed in our *Reporter*. I enclose a copy of these as you may like to translate them into Portuguese and make use of them.

With regard to your letter I should very much like to be able to obtain its insertion in *The Times* or, failing that, one of the other papers, but as you are fully aware the Irish coach now stops the way. Meanwhile we are having your letter put up in type with one or two *very slight* verbal alterations for the sake of euphony, though I must assure you that your English is very nearly as good as an Englishman's. In fact it is a great deal better than many of us can write.

When there is a little lull in the political world I will try whether any of the papers are open to the insertion of your letter. Meanwhile I send you a copy of a Report on Morocco, in case the one forwarded you by last month's mail should have miscarried.

We are trying very hard to have the seat of the British Legation removed from the coast to the interior, as the first step towards opening the country to civilisation.

We have had a very long and wearisome winter in England; indeed few

84 Henry Brougham, first Lord Brougham (1778–1868), scientist, lawyer, Whig politician and abolitionist who, as Lord Chancellor in Lord Grey's government 1830–4, was responsible for the passage of the 1832 Reform Act and the Act of 1833 abolishing slavery throughout the British empire. The eloquent words referred to were probably:

> Tell me not of rights, talk not of the property of the planter in his slaves. I deny the right. I acknowledge not the property. The principles, the feelings of our common nature, rise in rebellion against it . . . There is a law above all the enactments of human codes – the same throughout the world, the same in all times . . . It is the law written by the finger of God on the heart of man; and by that law, unchangeable and eternal… men shall reject with indignation the wild and guilty fantasy that man can hold property in man.

persons remember any more disagreeable and inclement season, as for some months the sun was almost invisible. We have had much harder frosts but when there is sunshine these are not so trying to health.

Mrs. Allen has not been at all well, but with the present change in the weather she is getting all right. Neither of us are so young as we used to be. Still we both hope to live to see the slaves set free in Brazil and to welcome you to England, crowned with victory.

Believe me
Yours very truly
Chas. H. Allen

Letter 67
Nabuco to Allen

Monday [April 1887]
32 Grosvenor Gardens

Dear Mr. Allen

I arrived yesterday in London and am staying with Baron de Penedo. If I possibly can I will call on you today; if not to-morrow or the day after. I hope and trust that my present voyage to Europe and I hope too to the United States will be of some advantage to the cause of the slaves. Slavery is *reduced* in Brazil to a term of thirteen years, but that is not a reason to stop condemning it and asking for its immediate overthrow, on the contrary. Last year I was not in Parliament, but in the daily press, writing in the columns of *O Paiz* have done probably more for our cause than I could have done as a deputy. In fact it was through the press that we forced the Conservative Cabinet to pass the law abolishing flogging, which if we had judges and the laws with regard to slaves were a reality, would amount practically to the end of slavery, a little too in the fashion which you once suggested me, of doing with it as it was done in India. Since it is not *lawful* to flog slaves, I do not know how the masters could enforce their *rights* on them.

I wish you could send me a copy of the *Reporter* that contains my article on Mr. Goldwin Smith's opinions [August–September 1886]. I received a letter of thanks from Mr. Garrison of New York, but did not see the article.

Hoping to see you soon and to be kindly remembered to Mrs. Allen, I remain
Very sincerely yours
Joaquim Nabuco

Letter 68
Allen to Nabuco

21 April 1887
13 Well Walk, Hampstead

My dear Senhor Nabuco

When I told Mrs. Allen you had been as good to bring her a parrot she was extremely pleased, and said she could not have received a more acceptable present. I therefore write a line to accept it on her behalf and to thank you from her.

You must let me send up for it.

We hope you will soon be able to fix a day to come and see us quietly in our new home. We are close to the Heath – at least within a minute's walk, and it is our own house, so we are settled in perhaps for the rest of our days.

Do you remember I once asked General Gordon to come and meet you at Highgate? Unfortunately he did not come. I am glad you saw the African Missionary[85] this afternoon.

Believe me yours very sincerely
Chas. H. Allen

85 Unidentified.

Letter 69
Allen to Nabuco

23 April 1887
55 New Broad Street

My dear Senhor Nabuco

The enclosed has come from Ryde [Isle of Wight].[86] Can you help me to answer it? I fancy this must be the Company that was in Chancery and to dispose of which Mr. Williams was sent out. I believe he is still there – but we do not know what became of the Negroes.

Did the Court of Chancery sell the slaves? And if so, what right had they as Englishmen to become slave-dealers? Any information at your leisure will be esteemed a favour by

Yours very truly
Chas. H. Allen

86 Unidentified.

Letter 70
Allen to Nabuco

13 June 1887
55 New Broad Street

My dear Senhor

The enclosed has come, from Mr. Stead.[87] Perhaps you would like to call on Thursday and then you could come on here afterwards and go home with me.

Nothing from Mr. Gladstone yet but I wrote to him on Friday.

Yours very truly
Chas. H. Allen

87 Unidentified.

Letter 71
Allen to Nabuco

14 June 1887
55 New Broad Street

Dear Senhor

Mr. Gladstone invites you and me to come to his wife's garden party at Dollis Hill at 4.30 on Friday next 18th inst.

The state of his voice obliges him to decline 'conversational interviews' but you will get some little opportunity I dare say. Will you be *here* by 3 and we will go together by train?

If you will send me a line by return. I will accept for us both.

Yours sincerely
Chas. H. Allen

Letter 72
Alexander to Nabuco

19 July [1887]
12 Old Square, Lincoln's Inn, London W.C.

Dear Senhor Nabuco

Enclosed please find programme of our conference next week. I suppose you have received a ticket for the Mansion House on Monday evening.

Mr. Allen rather hopes to raise a discussion on the 3rd question down for Wednesday pm, with regard to Emir Pasha's position in Central Africa,[88] but I don't know whether you would be prepared to take part in this. If so, it would be very satisfactory to the Anti Slavery Committee. The *Association* will of course be pleased for you to take part in the discussion of *any* subject which you take an interest.

Hoping to meet you, I am
Yours very truly
Joseph. G. Alexander

Thank you very much for you kind offer. Please reserve yourself for a *conversazione* at the Drapers' Hall on Friday evening, and a reception at the Attorney-General's on Wednesday evening.

88 Emir Pasha, born Eduard Schnitzer, in Silesia (1840–92), African explorer and adventurer who collaborated in the German penetration of Africa.

Letter 73
Nabuco to Allen

16 September 1887
Pernambuco

Dear Mr. Allen

I was elected yesterday here by a vote of 1,407 against 1,270 given to the Minister of the Empire, namely by a majority of 137!

It is a tremendous victory for our cause, such a defeat of the Government in the person of one of his leading members.

From the last election we had a gain of 659 votes.

Right of public meeting was suspended, a meeting was dispersed by the cavalry one man being killed and several wounded, the greatest pressure was put on the public functionaries, bribery with public moneys was largely employed, and still the result was the crushing defeat of the Minister – such a victory being a new departure in our life – a grand new event in our history!

I congratulate the friends of Abolition on our triumph.

It is impossible to give you an idea of the enthusiasm that this act of independence and abnegation of the Pernambuco electorate is causing throughout the country!

Yours very truly
J. Nabuco

Letter 74
Allen to Nabuco

7 October 1887
55 New Broad Street

Dear Mr. Nabuco

Your letter of 16th inst from Pernambuco [letter 73] was received by me on the 2nd October, and I immediately forwarded it to *The Times* which inserted it on the following day.[89] I trust you will not be annoyed at my having thus made it public, as it seemed a pity that the good news should not be known. I have sent a copy of your letter to Mr. Gladstone, feeling sure that he would rejoice in the success of his late visitor, in whom he took so much interest. It is not necessary to say that you have the warmest sympathy of all the Abolitionists of England, and I am directed by our Committee to forward you Copy of Minute unanimously passed at their meeting this day [7 October].[90] Please accept also sincere congratulations of Mrs. Allen and my family, in which I heartily join.

---

89 Allen's letter to *The Times*, 3 October, published 4 October:

Sir

Some months ago one of the members for Pernambuco received an appointment as Minister of the Crown, and his seat thus became vacant, the Brazilian law requiring a re-election, as in this country. Our friend, Senhor Joaquim Nabuco, the leader of the abolition movement in Brazil, who was in England at the time, immediately took his passage to Pernambuco in order to contest the election and endeavour to win from his opponent the seat which he has more than once held in the Brazilian Parliament. This apparently forlorn hope has, I am pleased to state, resulted in the triumph of the abolition cause, and as Senhor Nabuco's election is of interest to all those who have the true welfare of the Empire at heart, I ask the favour of your insertion of the following letter, which I have this morning received from him . I am, Sir, yours faithfully, Charles H. Allen.

Both letters were reprinted in the *Anti-Slavery Reporter* September–October 1887.

90 The Committee have learned with deep satisfaction that the prompt and vigorous action taken by Senhor JOAQUIM NABUCO in proceeding to Brazil at a few days' notice to contest the seat formerly held by him in Pernambuco now rendered vacant by the acceptance of a Ministerial appointment by the late holder, has been crowned with success. The Committee recognise the fact that the election of Senhor NABUCO on an Abolition platform by a large majority over the Government candidate, is an important step in the progress of emancipation in Brazil, and is calculated to hasten the day when the abominable system of Slavery shall be extirpated by the people of that Empire.

Published in the *Anti-Slavery Reporter* September–October 1887

My wife and I have been spending five very happy weeks in Switzerland mostly in the Upper [illegible]. 6,000 feet above the sea. The pure bright air of this elevated region, and the mostly unclouded sun have had a very beneficial effect upon our health, and will, I trust, enable us better to endure the rigours of our English winter. I forwarded you two copies of *The Times* containing your letter to me, one to Pernambuco, and the other to Rio de Janeiro, both of which will, I trust, arrive safely. At present we have received no Brazilian paper with comments upon your re-election, although probably they will arrive next mail.

With all good wishes,
Believe me
Yours very sincerely
Chas. H. Allen

'Papagai' is very well and handsome and is getting quite tame – but he does not yet speak.

Letter 75
Allen to Nabuco

1 November 1887

Dear Senhor Nabuco

By the last mail but one I had the pleasure of forwarding copy of a minute passed by this Committee congratulating you upon the success of your spirited contest in Pernambuco. I also sent you two copies of *The Times* containing your letter in it [to me] announcing the fact. I have now the pleasure to send you copy of extract from letter of Rt. Hon. W. E. Gladstone to me acknowledging my letter to him, announcing your success.

> *'Hawarden, Oct. 8th, 1887'*
> *I learn with the most cordial satisfaction the intelligence of Senhor Nabuco's election, which you have been kind enough to send me, and I would beg you, if you have an opportunity to convey to him my sincere congratulations'.*

We have lately received a visit from the Rev. E. Vanorden of Rio Grande do Sul, one of our Corresponding members. This gentleman informs us that there is a general desire among planters to substitute European immigration for the present system of slave labour.[91] The question arises as to what is to become of the slaves, if, when set free, they are not to be allowed to work for wages. Also, what guarantee is there, that immigrants from Europe will be certain to receive proper protection, and fair treatment?

It appears to us that the Italians are the only Europeans likely to stand the climate. We have heard reports that many of those immigrants have been reduced to great straits and were thoroughly disappointed in their expectations.

I send you by book post a Consular Report on this subject by Consul Ricketts,[92] and the Committee would be very glad to have your opinion, not only upon the progress of Emancipation in Brazil, but also of the probability of European labour eventually superseding that of the blacks. We have a lively recollection of the mistake formerly made in our own colonies by the planters who, because the negro refused to work for a miserable pittance of about 2/- [two shillings] a week, turned him out on a plea that he was lazy. Our experience is that some check must be put upon the planters, or else what is to become of the negro?

---

91 Between 1884 and 1887 145,880 European immigrants, the majority Italians, entered Brazil. In 1888, the year in which slavery was finally abolished, a further 132,000 Europeans arrived, making abolition more acceptable to the slave-owners.

92 Report on slavery in Brazil by George Thorne Ricketts, consul in Rio de Janeiro, published in the *Anti Slavery Reporter*, September–October 1887.

With all best wishes
Believe me yours very sincerely, [Allen]
Mrs Allen and family join me in kind remembrances. Also Papagai.

Letter 76
Sturge to Nabuco

21 December 1887
Charlbury, Oxon

Dear Senhor

I thank you for your letter of yesterday's date.[93]

On the matter of the address to the Pope[94] I have today written to Mr. Allen, that I think it should contain an historical reference to those occasions on which popes or cardinals have acted or written on the slave trade and slavery from the time of Cardinal Ximenes and since. But I have also said that a direct deputation from our Committee to the Pope which would be published everywhere would greatly detract from the spontaneous character which a declaration from the head of the Catholic church should bear.

I shall learn from Mr. Allen your views as to what can be done in the United States and the West Indies. Do you visit them as you return? If so I would suggest your calling at Cuba – it has just finished the course of abolition, which Brazil is now beginning.[95]

Yours very truly
Edmund Sturge

---

93 Letter not found.

94 1888 was the fiftieth anniversary of Pope Leo XIII's ordination as a priest. Various Brazilian bishops had appealed to Catholics in pastoral letters to offer, in honour of the Pope, the liberation of their slaves. At this time, Princess Isabel became regent in the absence of the emperor in Europe for medical treatment. The princess was well known for her deep religiosity. It occurred to Nabuco that she might not be able to resist an appeal from the Pope in favour of abolition. He decided, with the help of the British and Foreign Anti-Slavery Society, which secured letters of recommendation from Cardinal Manning (see note 96), to visit the Pope. The two met – alone, conversing in French – on 10 February 1888. The Pope promised to say 'a word' against slavery, adding that 'when the Pope has spoken, all Catholics have to obey'. The Cotegipe government managed to delay the publication of the Pope's encyclical which only came out after abolition. But news of the meeting between the Pope and Nabuco and the content of their conversation circulated widely in Brazil. See Carolina Nabuco, *Life of Joaquim Nabuco* ([1929] Stanford, 1950), pp.16–3.

95 Spain had freed children born of slave mothers and slaves over 60 in Cuba and Puerto Rico in 1870 and abolished slavery in Puerto Rico in 1873. In 1880 slavery was abolished in Cuba but initially with an eight-year period of 'tutelage' (*patronato*). Slavery was finally abolished in Cuba in October 1886.

Letter 77
Allen to Nabuco

4 January 1888
55 New Broad Street

My dear Senhor

The letters from the Cardinal[96] having arrived so promptly after my application, I think it is better to send them on to you *in Paris*. Please send a *carte postale* saying you have received them.

With all good wishes for the success of your Pontifical journey.

I am your sincerely
Chas. H. Allen

96 Cardinal Henry Edward Manning (1807–92), a High Anglican who had converted to Catholicism in 1851, became Archbishop of Westminster (head of Catholic Church in England) in 1865 and a Cardinal 1875. He had progressive views on social justice which influenced Pope Leo XIII.

Letter 78
Allen to Nabuco

13 January 1888

My dear Senhor

The enclosed has been returned thro the P.O. having missed you. I fancy you may like to see it.

I am glad you received the Cardinal's letters safely in Paris.

The Committee would not let me go to Rome – but I hope you are getting on all right.

We have had fearful fogs and I have been obliged to stay mostly at home. Nothing yet of yours in *The Times* and no letter from the Editor so I know nothing. Let us know when to expect you back. Mr. Sturge hopes you will go to Cuba.

Yours very truly
Chas H. Allen

Letter 79
Allen to Nabuco

17 January 1888
17 Well Walk, Hampstead

Dear Senhor Nabuco

Many thanks for your letter from Rome dated 12th inst.[97] I wrote you a few lines to the address you gave us there some days ago – enclosing the letter I sent you to Brazil, which had been sent back through the Post Office.

I am very glad the Pope's Secretary of State[98] is so good to you, for he can help you a great deal. I see the Pope has canonized Peter Claver[99] and two others, but no mention was made of Peter Claver's anti-slavery work. Of course as a Protestant this ceremony has to me no meaning or value, but I hope you will be able to obtain from the Pope the promise to issue a Bull which will influence *living* men and induce them to set their slaves free. There would be something tangible in that – but men who have been dead 300 years have passed out of the sphere of this world and I cannot conceive how they themselves can be affected by anything done to their memory by any man still living here. I do not think it would be wise for me to write to *The Times* about your MS.[100] for the Editor may still intend to publish it. When you return here if it has not been used it might be well for *you* to write and let him know what you have done in Rome and then ask for the MS. – I thought Teall made this from your copy, so he might write it over again if necessary. We have had dreadful weather since you left. A thick fog for nearly a week and then a cruel icy east wind, which still continues. I have been confined to the house many days and am still at home a prisoner.

We all unite in wishing you a Happy New year and a very successful mission at the Papal Court.

Believe me, Yours very truly
Chas. H. Allen
Papagai is very flourishing and bears his or her first winter in England very well.

97 Letter not found.

98 Cardinal Rampolla. Nabuco met him on 11 January, the day he arrived in Rome. It was a month before he met the Pope (on 10 February, see notes 91 and 92).

99 Peter Claver, Catalan Jesuit priest (1581–1654). From 1610 to his death in 1654 in Cartagena, Claver baptised and instructed in the faith several hundred thousand African slaves (hence 'the apostle of the negroes'). He was beatified by Pope Pius IX in 1850 and canonised by Pope Leo XIII on 15 January 1888.

100 MS unknown. Allen did in the event write to the editor (see letter 81).

Letter 80
Allen to Nabuco

23 January 1888
55 New Broad Street

Dear Nabuco

Nothing yet in *The Times*. Mr. Sturge thinks that if you could get *The Times* Correspondent in Rome to send a notice of your mission to the Pope and an explanation of the Jubilee emancipation movement in Brazil[101] it would quicken the movements of those in Printing House Sq. Can you do this? I have had a long paper sent to me by the F.O. *to read and return*. It is from the British Consul, Mr. Gough, dated Rio December 12 and he says emancipation is proceeding apace.

Mrs. Allen has made a copy for you to see when you return.

Hoping all is going on well
I am yours truly
Chas. H. Allen

101 This refers to the action of the Brazilian bishops mentioned in note 94 above.

Letter 81
Allen to Nabuco

25 March 1888
17 Well Walk, Hampstead

Dear Senhor Nabuco

We are all very sorry to hear that you have so bad a cold – but hope with careful nursing you will soon lose it. I do not wonder you were affected by the change from the blue skies of Italy to the dull cold atmosphere of this East windy isle. If the weather were more genial I would do myself the pleasure of calling upon you but I have been almost a prisoner to the house all this week.

We all hope that before you leave London the weather will be milder and that you will be able to come here and take a family meal with us, as before. We have told Mr. Sturge that we should like him to come to meet you here next week, as that is his week in London. Our Committee meeting is next Friday at 3.30 so perhaps you will look in at the Office then and say goodbye to the Members. If you are well enough on Wednesday or Thursday I should think either of those days should suit Mr. Sturge to meet you here. We are all anxious to hear about your interview with the Holy Father. I am disgusted with *The Times* and think it is not very gentlemanly conduct and take no notice of all our communications. Mr. Buckle[102] promised to give his best consideration of your paper, so I sent it with a private introductory letter, nearly two months ago! No reply.

Then I sent him your letter written to me from Rome showing that you expected the MS back if it was not used, and he has not replied to my letter nor returned me yours. The late Editor, Mr. Chenery[103] always treated me with more courtesy.

You would hear from Mr. Teall that I have been out of health all the winter. I suffer chiefly from insomnia, which is a very trying complaint. One gets so tired of lying awake hour after hour.

In about a fortnight I expect to go to Egypt, as the doctor has ordered me a sea voyage. Probably I shall not stay there more than a week or so – as the object is the voyage. I wish I could go with you to Brasil!

Your beautiful parrot is perfectly well and seems to enjoy his first winter in England. We cover his cage at night and keep him very snug and warm. He is wonderfully tame and very impudent. My daughters dote upon him – they say *I* do also.

---

102 George Earle Buckle, editor, 1884–1912.

103 Thomas Chenery, editor, 1877–84.

Trusting that you will be able to give us the pleasure of your company next week.

I am, Yours sincerely
Chas. H Allen

Letter 82
Allen to Nabuco

16 May 1888
55 New Broad Street

My dear Nabuco

It is impossible for me to find the words sufficiently strong and impressive in our poor nothern tongue, to convey to you the pleasure and heartfelt congratulations, which we all desire to offer you on the accomplishment of the great work of Liberation to which you and your good Father before you had devoted your lives.[104]

The telegram on Saturday last, briefly announced that 'The Brazilian Chamber of Deputies had voted the immediate and unconditional abolition of Slavery in Brazil'. Then in a few days we heard that the Senate had confirmed it, that the heart of the dying Emperor had beat with fresh vigour at the great news which had been flashed across the waters of the broad Atlantic – that ocean over which, in days gone by, so many thousands of Africans had been born[e] to feed the greed of the Planters of Brazil. I am glad the good old Monarch has lived to see this day. What the effect will be on the mighty army of bondsmen it is too early to predict, but I believe the Slaves will fall into their proper place under the new conditions with very little disturbance of the equilibrium of the Empire. My first impulse was to telegraph you the congratulations of this Society, but as it would have cost about 4 pounds I had to forego this luxury and content myself with the slower postal route. You would know that we rejoice in your success and thank God for this great victory.

I am writing these few lines to go by the first Mail that may be starting before our regular mail and I hope you will receive these without any delay.

The *Reporter* also goes herewith. You will see I have been to Egypt in which country a work of emancipation is gradually going on. I trust I may live to see

104 The Cotegipe cabinet had resisted pressure from Princess Isabel to adopt further abolitionist measures. On 10 March 1888 Cotegipe resigned and was replaced by senator João Alfredo Correia de Oliveira, a progressive Conservative committed to the cause of abolition. On 8 May the new government presented a bill for the abolition of slavery to the chamber which, at the request of Nabuco, dispensed with its normal timetable and approved it the next day by 83 votes to nine. On 11 May the bill was presented to the senate where Dantas requested that the normal rules be suspended in the interests of its speedy passage; the bill was approved the next day with only six votes against. On 13 May the princess regent returned to Rio from Petrópolis to sign the Lei Áurea – in the midst of immense popular celebrations which lasted a week. See Introduction and Chronology.

all Slavery put down in Egypt as it is in Brazil. *Now* no Christian power holds any slaves and the abomination is left for Mohammedans and heathens to carry out. This is a great advance in moral and religious progress and in time the Mohammedans must follow so good an example.

At our next Committee Meeting in June some Minute will be officially passed to word this great event of Emancipation in Brazil,[105] but meanwhile you will, I hope, safely receive this message of hearty congratulation on behalf of all English Anti-Slavery people, many of whom have not yet realized how great is the boon which the Brazilian Parliament has given to the world. It ought to inspire the soul of the Old Poet of Freedom, the Quaker, Whittier,[106] and make him chronicle the great event in lines of fire.

Mrs. Allen and my family join me in personal congratulations to yourself – the 'Coeur de Lion' that has so long led the 'forlorn hope' of the army of

105 On 29 May Allen sent minister Penedo a copy of a Resolution passed on 23 May (see letter 83 below).

On 1 June the society sent an Address to Nabuco himself:

> The Committee of the British and Foreign Anti-Slavery Society offer **Senhor Joaquim Nabuco** their hearty congratulations upon the happy attainment of the life-long aspirations of his late honoured Father, and of himself, by the happy completion of their long-continued and unflinching labours in the cause of human freedom.
> THE ABOLITION OF SLAVERY IN BRAZIL, so peacefully and triumphantly obtained, is the crowning stone of that great edifice built up by Christian Nations, as a perpetual memorial of the equal rights of men, of whatsoever colour or nation.
> It is with feelings of thankfulness and satisfaction that the Committee see the last blot on the escutcheon of Christianity wiped out for ever by the noble action of Brazil.
> The Committee would ask SENHOR NABUCO kindly to convey to those ILUSTRIOUS COLLEAGUES who have assisted him in the great work to which he and they have devoted their lives, the expression of their warmest appreciation of the noble services rendered by the ABOLITIONIST PARTY IN BRAZIL to the cause of humanity.
> They pray that the fruits of this great Acct of Emancipation may be seen in the long course of peaceful prosperity to that great Empire over which HIS MAJESTY THE EMPEROR is, by the Grace of God, still permitted to reign.
> On behalf of the committee,
> Arthur Pease, President, Edmund Sturge, Chairman, Joseph Allen, Treasurer, Chas. H. Allen, Secretary.

Published in the *Anti-Slavery Reporter*, July–August 1888.

106 John Greenleaf Whittier (1807–92), American poet and abolitionist. Whittier met emperor Pedro II during his visit to the United States in 1876. He wrote a poem on the law of free birth (1871), 'The cry of a lost soul', which was translated by the emperor as 'O choro d'uma alma perdida'.

freedom and has now given the thundering blow that has burst asunder the last iron link in the chain of Slavery. Hurrah! and Te Deum Laudamus.

Very sincerely yours
Chas. H. Allen

Letter 83
Allen to Penedo

29 May 1888

Sir

I have the honour to forward [a] copy of a Resolution passed at a meeting of the Members of the Anti Slavery Society on Wednesday last the 23rd inst.[107] The success of the Abolition Movement in Brazil has afforded unfeigned satisfaction to the Members of this Society, and on their behalf I ask Your Excellency to be good enough to forward to His Imperial Majesty the Emperor the enclosed Resolution together with the letter accompanying it.

With the expression of my high consideration and esteem, I have the honour to be,

Your Excellency's faithful servant,
Chas. H. Allen

107 The resolution (not located) was sent to the emperor by Penedo. But it did not receive a reply. See letter 86 below.

Letter 84
Lady Buxton[108] to Nabuco

3 June 1888
Colne House, Cromer

Dear Signor Nabuco

I must tell you how greatly interested I am in this fine news from Brazil – the end of Slavery!

I heartily congratulate you on the success of your noble efforts and thank God that he raised you up and led you on to such a victory. It reminds me of the life and efforts of my dear father in law – the first Sir T Fowell Buxton. We shall anxiously watch the results and earnestly hope the black population will rise to the privileges of change in a fine Christian spirit.

You will still have much to call forth your powers of exertion and I pray God you may be sustained by His own Spirit working in you and for you.

My son Sir Fowell and myself have rejoiced together with other members of my family. Believe me

Your sincere friend
Catherine Buxton

108 Wife of Sir Thomas Fowell Buxton, daughter-in-law of the first Sir Thomas Fowell Buxton.

Letter 85
Sturge to Nabuco

15 June 1888

Dear Sen Nabuco

I have to thank you much for your letter of the 8th inst. confirming the telegrams published in our newspapers, and followed by your letter to Mr. Allen of a week later date.[109]

It is indeed a sudden and glorious consummation of your labours which you have pursued so long and unremittingly. In one point it far surpasses the act of emancipation of the slaves in the British West Indies, in that it ignored the question of compensation altogether, as was also done in Cuba. When that act passed in 1833, I remember that the compensation was strongly opposed by a large section of the antislavery party and the result soon proved that this part of the measure was a disastrous mistake. The money was received by the merchants to whom most of the sugar estates were heavily mortgaged; and these having received the whole or the partial amount of their debts refused any longer to make the usual advance of money for the cultivation of the ensuing crops. The consequence was the very general cessation of sugar cultivation, and an extensive demoralization of all industrial habit in the negro, from absolute want of employment. The industrial condition of Jamaica and other West India Islands has not been restored to this day.

Can you not at some future time write a 'History of abolition in Brazil'? It is an example that ought not be lost to the world.

We have now to be thankful for the extinction of both the slave trade and slavery throughout the Western World, but still alas for Africa and the Mohammedan East where the slave hunting Arabs are extending their devastations in Africa.

It is gratifying to learn from your letter that you[r] princess Imperial has taken a prominent interest in the matter, the more so that when we had an interview with her father, many years ago, the subject of emancipation did not seem on[e] that was welcome to him.

I remain
Yours very truly
Edmund Sturge

109 Neither Nabuco's letter to Sturge of 8 May nor Nabuco's letter to Allen of 13 May were located.

Letter 86
Allen to Nabuco

20 June 1888
55, New Broad Street

My dear Senhor

On the 16th May I wrote you an unofficial congratulatory letter [letter 82] respecting the glorious tidings of Emancipation in Brazil, in which I stated that I was sure the Committee would pass a Minute congratulating you on the attainment of this great object. Copy of that Minute, written on vellum, in order that you may be able to keep it for the rest of your life, goes out by this Mail in a tube, and I am assured at the Post Office that it is allowable to send it by Book Post. It will also be 'registered' and addressed to you in Rio de Janeiro, so that should you not receive it with this letter kindly enquire for it. You will see by the *Reporter* a copy of the address to the Emperor, duplicate copy of which is enclosed in the tube with your Minute. Please let us know when you safely receive these, and should the Post Office make any surcharge I will refund it to you.

I have just received your letter dated Rio May 13th[110] which you mark 'private'. I can well understand that you 'have no words to describe what you feel'.

I forwarded your letter to Mr. Sturge, but I have not seen it; he has written to you by this mail [letter 85]. I have also addressed a letter for you from the Dowager Lady Buxton [letter 84].

We have not yet seen any full report of your speech nor the incidents that accompanied the passing of the Bill, but of course we have seen the summary given by the *Rio News*. Some day I trust we may have full details.

The address to the Emperor was forwarded through Baron Penedo about 3 weeks ago, but at present we have received no acknowledgement. I enclosed with it a congratulatory letter to the Ambassador [letter 83].

We are all anxiously watching the effect of this great Emancipation Movement on Brazil. The policy lately adopted by that Empire being what we have always advocated with regard to slavery, viz, immediate and unconditional emancipation.

The £20,000,000 given to the West Indian planters was not approved of by the Anti Slavery Society and the result of such policy was by no means beneficial to the Colonies, though it enriched individuals, many of whom were mere money lenders, the estates being heavily mortgaged.

110 Letter not located.

My wife and family desire to join me in sincere congratulations and with our united kind regards

Believe me
Yours sincerely
Chas. H. Allen

Letter 87
Rebouças[111] to Sturge

10 July 1888
Rio de Janeiro

Dear Sir

I beg to hand you the number of *O Paiz* with a quotation of your estimable letter to my friend Joaquim Nabuco [letter 85].

This important topic was published exactly in the day of the discussion of a bill of indemnisation proposed by Cotegipe in favour of the ancient slave-holders.

So its effect was excellent and all the Brazilian abolitionists are very grateful to you for your good assistance in so momentous questions.

With my best compliments I remain, my dear Sir
Yours sincerely
André Rebouças
Member of the Anti-Slavery Society

111 André Rebouças (1838–1898), engineer and abolitionist, had been the first treasurer of the Sociedade Brasileira contra Escravidão when it was formed in September 1880. See letter 7.

Letter 88
Allen to Nabuco

7 November 1888

My dear Senhor

Since I last had the pleasure of addressing you a great deal has happened with regard to the East African slave trade. The two *Reporters* July – August, September – October, will show you how busy we have been in following up the good effects produced by Cardinal Lavigerie's great oration in July last.[112] The great interest taken by the Pope in this question is no doubt in part owing to your visit to His Holiness last winter when you impressed upon him the necessity for the Church speaking out upon the subject of slavery. With this letter I forward you a letter to the Princess Regent from our Society, which I trust you will do us the favour to present to Her Imperial Highness.[113] It may

---

112 Charles Martial Allemand Lavigerie (1825–92). Born in France, he became archbishop of Algiers in 1866 and cardinal in 1882. He dedicated himself to the promotion of Catholicism in the Muslim world and, with the support of Pope Leo XIII, to combating the slave trade and slavery in Africa.

113 Address presented to the princess regent by Nabuco and André Rebouças (see letter 89):

Madam,

The BRITISH AND FOREIGN ANTI-SLAVERY SOCIETY, which has already had the honour of addressing its congratulations to your August Father, on the great event of emancipation in Brazil, now begs leave respectfully to approach your Imperial Highness. The Society has, since the passing of the great Law of Abolition, No. 3353, of 13th May 1888, signed by your Highness, carefully watched the progress of events in the vast empire of Brazil. It is well aware that the passing of that law was, in a great measure, due to the great tact and firmness shown by your Imperial Highness; and there can be little doubt that the peaceful carrying out of the great programme inaugurated by that law, is also largely owing to the attachment which the people have ever felt towards the daughter of the illustrious house of Braganza, who, during the absence of the Emperor, held with so firm, yet gentle a hand, the reins of Government in Brazil.

The Society, therefore, offers its congratulations to your Imperial Highness upon this great and crowning act of emancipation, the carrying out of which not only frees the Continent of America from the stigma of Slavery – but inscribes the name of the PRINCESS REGENT DONA ISABEL, in the pages of history, amongst the noblest benefactors of the human race.

On the behalf of the BRITISH AND FOREIGN ANTI-SLAVERY SOCIETY, I have the honour to be, with much respect,

Edmund Sturge, Chairman, Joseph Allen, Treasurer, Chas. H. Allen, Secretary

appear rather late but we were anxious to watch the effect of emancipation in Brazil, and I thought we might have also received, ere this, an acknowledgement of the letter sent to the Emperor – perhaps it never reached him.

We shall be happy to hear from you how affairs progress in the Empire. I hope and expect to find that increased prosperity will be the result of the generous emancipation policy. The demands of some planters for compensation appear to us to be wrong in principle, and they will, I hope, be successfully resisted.

Mrs Allen and I have had a pleasant visit to Switzerland during the autumn, but we are now feeling the effects of the fogs and cold East winds which have set in already. Neither in England nor Europe has there been much summer this year, and I think you would scarcely have enjoyed it had you been here.

When shall you be coming over again? Mr. Sturge keeps well in spite of his 80 years, and most of the Committee appear to be in good health.

With all good wishes
Chas. H. Allen

The ladies desire [sic] their kind regards. Mary is in Portugal – Papaguy is very well – and quite tame. He does not talk.

Published in the *Anti-Slavery Reporter*, January–February 1889.

Letter 89
Nabuco to Allen

8 January 1889
Rio de Janeiro

Dear Mr. Allen

I had the honour of presenting the Anti-Slavery address to Her Imperial Highness who received me for that purpose in deputation with Mr. Rebouças, Mr. Gusmão Lobo another correspondent of the Society not being able to be present. Her Highness asked me to send your Society her hearty thanks for the sentiments you expressed to her.

I am not going this year to Europe. Strange to say the slave-owners have declared themselves, in large numbers, adverse to the throne and we have now an important republican faction to contend with. It was a very daring, bold thing, what the Princess did but I trust in God she will not lose her throne for it.[114]

After all you did not come to Brazil during the slavery period, will you come now? Only the crossing would do you good.

Many kind messages for a happy New Year to your family no. 1 and to the Society, your family no. 2.

Your sincere friend
Joaquim Nabuco

114 It is said that Cotegipe, after the approval of the Lei Áurea, declared to princess Isabel that she had redeemed a race but lost a throne [*redimira uma raça, mas perdera um trono*]. Nabuco himself saw clearly the negative impact of the law on the future of the monarchy. In a letter to Penedo on 25 May 1888 he wrote: 'I see the monarchy in serious danger, virtually doomed [*condenada*]. The Princess has become very popular, but the powerful [*poderosas*] reject her and the landowners are republican' (*Cartas aos amigos*, pp. 171–2). The republic was proclaimed on 15 November 1889.

II
Correspondence 1899–1902

Letter 1
Allen to Nabuco

18 March 1899
17 Well Walk, Hampstead

Dear Senhor Nabuco

Your letter of 8th December[1] was as unexpected as it was welcome, for it seemed such a very long time since I heard any voice from Brazil. It was indeed very pleasant to find how warmly you appreciated my poor work on behalf of the slave, and what a kindly remembrance you had of our joint efforts to procure abolition, not only in Brazil, but in other parts of the world. My wife and all my young people were delighted with your letter which was so full of eloquence, and of a rhythmical English that even natives seldom attain to. My Committee were very pleased to hear it read to them by my successor, Mr Buxton, and they would like to order a copy of the volumes containing the life of your Father if they are published in English or French. They must be very interesting and will no doubt give a history of slavery in Brazil that will be of the highest value, especially to the younger generation to whom it is now little more than a name. I often think of the visit we paid to Milan together to try to obtain from the Conference a declaration that the slave trade ought to be reckoned as piracy, when you will remember that Mr. Alexander – a member of our Committee – ably supported the cause which you so powerfully advocated. That same point was brought before the Congress of Verona in 1822 by an old cousin of mine, William Allen F.R.S., when the Duke of Wellington, who represented England, was strongly in favour of passing such a declaration. I believe it was lost by the action of France. How many of those with whom I worked are now dead – Joseph Cooper, Edmund Sturge, W. E. Forster, General Gordon, Lord Mayor Sir R.N. Fowler, Revd Horace Waller and many others. Then a final great loss cause came in Nov 97 when J. Eastoe Teall, who had always been my faithful assistant, and who knew more about the history of the slave-trade than anyone in England – died of dropsy at the early age of 41, having spent 22 years of his life in the office at 55 New Broad Street.

So much anxiety and extra work devolved upon me in the year 98 – Mr Teall having been incapacitated since early 97 – and dying after a long wearisome illness, that I felt the time had come for me to give up the single handed contest which I had maintained for a year and a half. I therefore gave in my resignation to our President Arthur Pease M.P. about May last year, and before it took effect in November he too had passed away from this world.

1 Letter not found.

I accepted the position of Honorary Secretary, having first been fortunate in securing the services of Mr. Travers Buxton as my successor and since then I have obtained the consent of his cousin Sir Fowell Buxton to take up the duties of President left vacant by the death of Arthur Pease.[2]

Yes our beloved and beautiful green parrot has departed 'without delivering the secret of his muteness'. He lived about 10 years with us and was the sweetest and most affectionate of pets. His devotion to me was quite extraordinary and I could do anything with him. When I had influenza he grew very sad and when he heard my voice upstairs he insisted upon being let out of the cage and then he climbed upstairs and on to my bed where he mounted on my shoulder and defied anyone to take him off. After that he spent the days in my room – as happy as a king! He was also very fond of my youngest daughter Beatrice, but everyone else had to take care not to come too near his terrible beak. He never spoke but I wrote an account of him which appeared in the *Spectator*. We have not yet ceased to miss our dearest pet, though it is nearly two years since we had to have him killed by prussic acid. He had struggled with great patience against a fungoid growth in the mouth which slowly penetrated into his throat and rendered eating too difficult and painful, for his end to be unduly prolonged.

We have another parrot – a grey one – given by a native of West Africa, nearly 10 years ago. He is a remarkable, jolly and healthy bird with a great facility in talking. But though he is very affectionate we are obliged to confine our attentions to scratching his poll. He is terrified at leaving his cage and we cannot handle him as we did your beautiful bird.

I am happy to say we are all well, considering our advancing years. I shall be 75 next month which is quite beyond the average. My youngest son is the only one married and he and his wife live close to us and as they have no children we often see them. My son is Assistant Secretary of the Technical Education Board, and though he is not highly paid, he has a great deal to do, but it is interesting work and his wife is delighted to cooperate with him in any way possible.

My two nieces whom you saw at Montevideo are well – Josephine, the elder, lives with her father at the sea-side and the other (Margaret) is married and has been to India for her honeymoon – but that is over long ago.

With our united kind regards to you and Madame, I am yours most sincerely

Chas H. Allen

2 Allen ceased to be secretary of the society and became honorary secretary in November 1898. Sir Fowell Buxton was the grandson of the abolitionist Sir Thomas Fowell Buxton.

I was glad to see in *The Times* your appointment to a high official post in an approaching arbitration.[3]

3 In January 1899 Brazil agreed to submit to the arbitration of King Victor Emmanuel III of Italy the territorial dispute with Great Britain over the boundaries of British Guiana. In March Nabuco was invited by Olinto de Magalhães, president Campos Sales' minister of foreign relations, to head a special mission in London entrusted with the task of preparing Brazil's case. He arrived in England at the end of May, but spent most of the following twelve months in Paris. On 23 March 1900 João Artur de Souza Corrêa, the Brazilian minister in London, suddenly died. Nabuco was immediately made envoy extraordinary and minister plenipotentiary in London, but at this stage still with responsibility for the British Guiana question only, not the Brazilian minister in London where Oliveira Lima was chargé d'affaires. In July Nabuco was finally appointed minister, presented his credentials to Queen Victoria on 13 December, and took over the Brazilian legation in February 1901, combining the post of Brazilian minister with that of Brazil's representative in the international arbitration over British Guiana.

Letter 2
Allen to Nabuco (c/o Joseph Allen)

28 May 1899
Teignmouth

Dear Mr Nabuco

A letter received from home this morning gave me the unexpected but most pleasing news that a beautiful green parrot – the facsimile of our departed favourite – had arrived at our house from the Brazilian Legation, as a present from you. It is so very kind of you to have taken the trouble to bring up another pet that I do not know how to thank you sufficiently for your kind thought. Mrs Allen and I are staying in South Devonshire though not at the same place, for she is at Torquay visiting her only remaining first cousin – an old lady of 80 – and I am staying with my brother, our Treasurer, whose daughter you saw in Montevideo, some years ago. Her uncle, with whom she was staying, is now British Minister in Japan.

Teignmouth is only 8 miles from Torquay by sea, but it is a troublesome journey by land, as you have to change trains at a junction and then have a cab for 2½ miles to our cousin's house. As I am confined to the house with a bronchial cold and dare not face these cold East winds, I have not seen my wife since we started from Paddington nearly a fortnight ago. Still I am quite sure she would heartily join me in welcoming you once more to our shores, especially as you come as a messenger of peace – in the matter of Brazil and British Guiana – and she would also heartily thank you for restoring to life – as it were – our lost Brazilian pet.

Our house is now being papered and painted etc., but in a fortnight I hope we shall be home, and trust we may have the pleasure of thanking you in person for your kind thought.

Believe me, yours very sincerely
Chas. H. Allen

Letter 3
Travers Buxton to Nabuco

6 February 1900
55 New Broad Street

My dear Sir

In view of the forthcoming International Anti-Slavery Congress which is arranged to be held in Paris in August next, this Society has been asked by the French Anti-Slavery Society to send representatives and to present papers on branches of the subject of which it has had experience.

The Committee has decided to ask certain Corresponding Members of the Society if they would be good enough to write papers of this character, and I am directed to make this request of you. The Committee feel that if you could see your way to write an account of the Anti-Slavery struggle in Brazil, it would be of very exceptional value and interest. I am sending a copy of the official programme of the Congress, in order that you may understand its character and scope.

I am, Sir, with much respect,
Your faithful servant
Travers Buxton
Secretary

Letter 4
Allen to Nabuco

9 February 1900
17 Well Walk, Hampstead,

My dear friend

I hope you received the letter I sent you last June [sic] [letter 2, 28 May] thanking you for so kindly bringing me another beautiful green parrot. Not having heard of or from you since I concluded you had returned to Brazil though I hesitated to send you the pamphlets concerning my resignation of the Secretaryship until I knew. As the Committee has now directed my successor to write to you requesting you to write a paper for the Anti-Slavery Conference at Paris, and it was sent to me to forward, I thought it better to address a note to the Legation to ask whether you had returned to Brazil. They inform me that you are still in Paris, therefore I forward Mr Buxton's letter and am also sending you by 'book post' my two resignation pamphlets and *also my photograph*, of which I pray your acceptance. I am now very much absolved from Anti-Slavery work during the present winter as we cannot do much whilst everyone is so preoccupied with the war in South Africa,[4] and I have no anxiety about funds, as the Society has just had a legacy of £2,000. This is more than it received from legacies during the 20 years I was there, and is a slice of luck for the new Secretary! You will be pleased to hear that the beautiful parrot has grown into a very fine bird. It is evidently quite young as he is so active and lively. He still calls himself 'papagai real' but has already picked up many English words and phrases. 'Polly put the kettle on' is his favourite little speech. My two daughters are extremely devoted to him and he readily comes out of the cage and sits on their hands. The grey African parrot looks on him with contempt. When you come to London you must come and see them and us. When will that be?

Excuse my coming on to Buxton's sheet but the post not allowing more than ½ an ounce I could not take further paper of my own.

You will I know be glad to learn that Mrs Allen and I have escaped influenza, though we had it in the house. It has been a cold foggy disagreeable winter and we now have a spell of hard frost 18°, 20° and 22° Fahrenheit – and snow still on the ground. I hope you have escaped the usual scourge and are well. I see you have it pretty cold in Paris.

4 The second Boer war, or South African war, October 1899–May 1902, in which Britain defeated the two independent Boer republics of Transvaal and the Orange Free State and incorporated them into the British empire in what became in 1910 the Union of South Africa.

By this post I send you the little packet alluded to but it may not be delivered with this letter. We are all absorbed in the war and feel the greatest confidence in Lords Roberts and Kitchener[5] and 'Joe' Chamberlain![6] The latter is the strongest man in the government and the proof of that is the vile abuse of him in French and German papers, and by the 'Rads' [Radicals] at home. I hope you see *The Times* for you cannot learn much that is true about the war from French papers. Mrs Allen joins me in kindest regards and good wishes.

Yours sincerely
Chas. H. Allen

5 Field Marshal Lord Roberts (1832–1914) was the commander of the British troops in the first phase of the Boer war. Lord Kitchener (1850–1916) succeeded Roberts in November 1900.

6 Joseph Chamberlain (1836–1914), business man and Liberal Unionist politician, was colonial secretary in the Conservative government of Lord Salisbury at the time of the Boer war.

Letter 5
Nabuco to Buxton

10 February 1900
Paris

Dear Sir

As I worked so cordially with the Anti-Slavery Society when fighting against Slavery in Brazil, and I had the privilege of representing it together with dear Mr. Allen at the Milan Congress of 1883, I am at your service for anything you think useful with regard to your noble and great cause. In this general answer is comprised the first demand you make for my services, to which I have great pleasure in complying. I am glad to see Mr. Allen had the privilege of having for his successor one of the patrician Abolitionist family of the Buxtons, who has inherited the spirit that made their name ever memorable.

I am, Sir,
Yours truly
Joaquim Nabuco

Letter 6
Allen to Nabuco

18 April 1900
17 Well Walk, Hampstead

Your Excellency
and very dear Sir

How very heartily we all congratulate you on your appointment as Minister for Brazil at the Court of St. James![7] And we consider also that Brazil herself is to be congratulated on having such a Representative in England.

In our last Committee meeting 6th April, I had seen a notice of your appointment in *The Times* of that day and I therefore proposed a Minute of which I now have the great pleasure to enclose a copy. It was, as you may well believe, carried unanimously, and as I have seen no notice of your further movements, I conclude you are in communication with the Legation here, and therefore forward the enclosed to that address. Mr. Buxton hopes you will still be able to write a paper for the Anti-Slavery Conference in Paris next August, and that possibly you may find it possible to attend in person.

In either case if may be of use if I send you a copy of the proceedings in Milan in 1883 when you kindly joined the Deputation from our Society and made a splendid oration in French.

With our united best wishes for your health and happiness and a long diplomatic career in London.
I am yours very sincerely
Chas. H. Allen

Committee meeting 6 April 1900, Sir T Fowell Buxton presiding
Copy of minute 927
The following *Resolution* was carried,
That this Committee having heard with pleasure that *Senhor Joaquim Nabuco has been appointed Minister for Brazil to the Court of St. James*, offers its hearty congratulations to the former President of the Anti-Slavery Society of Brazil, and assures him of the gratification which the news afforded to its members.

The Committee remembers with satisfaction the assistance given by Senhor Nabuco to the small delegation sent by the Society to the Conference on International Law at Milan in September 1883 when he delivered an eloquent

7 Nabuco had not in fact at this stage been appointed Brazilian minister in London (see letter 1), as he was quick to point out (see letters 7 and 8).

address on slavery and the slave trade. Senhor Nabuco's long and arduous labours in Brazil which eventually resulted in the emancipation of about a million slaves on 13th May 1888 still remain fresh in the memory of the Committee with whom Senhor Nabuco worked for so many years in perfect harmony and with such excellent results.

Letter 7
Nabuco to Allen

3 May 1900
Pau

Dear Mr. Allen,

Only one word to thank you and the committee for kind congratulations so heartily sent and which I now receive, I will answer officially when I find the constant moving from place to place of the last weeks at an end. But there is a misunderstanding in the news given. I have been appointed Envoy Extraordinary and Minister Plenipotentiary to England, it is true, but not to replace my friend Souza Corrêa, only on an Especial Mission, which cannot last long.[8] However it will give me immense pleasure to go back to London and find myself again near you, whose friendship is sweeter and sweeter while it grows older.

My kindest regards to Mrs. Allen and all yours and believe me, my dear and good friend,
Yours very truly
Joaquim Nabuco

8 See note to letter 1.

Letter 8
Nabuco to Allen

7 June 1900
Pouges les Eaux,

Dear Mr. Allen,

I beg you to convey to the Committee of the Anti-Slavery Society my deep sense of the honour done to me by its vote and my sincere appreciation of the recollection they keep of our old and friendly relations. At the same time I must inform you that it is not to the permanent post in London I have been appointed, but to an Extraordinary Mission.

I have the honour to be, dear Mr. Allen,
Yours sincerely
Joaquim Nabuco

Letter 9
Buxton to Nabuco

9 June 1900

My dear Sir

In your letter to me of February last you were so good as to comply with the request of my Committee to write a paper on Brazilian Slavery for presentation to the International Anti-Slavery Congress in Paris, to be held in August next.

May I ask if you can kindly forward me the paper at your early convenience, as my Committee has resolved to send in the papers which this Society is presenting with as little delay as possible.

We propose to have the papers translated into French, but I presume that the paper that you are contributing will be written in that language.

We are very sensible of your kindness in finding time to undertake this office on behalf of the society.

With much respect,
I beg to remain, Sir
Your faithful servant
Travers Buxton

Letter 10
Nabuco to Buxton

15 July 1900
St. Germain en Laye, Pavillon Louis XIV

Dear Sir,

I am sorry if I were to disappoint you, but I am not able to send the promised paper in time for the Congress, as the books I wanted for writing it are still delayed. What relieves my mind is that I hardly could treat, for want of special information, of the part your Society took in the struggle for the extinction of the slave-trade and slavery with us, which in a paper coming from it or under its *auspices*, ought to be a feature. I was a little discouraged too from writing as the list sent me by the organizers of the Congress only included subjects dealing with the pending questions and issues in your path, and not with historical subjects, such as the Abolition of Slavery in South or North America.

Meanwhile as I will do my best to be present to the meeting of the Congress, on account of your invitation and of the one I received from the organizers to represent Brazil, we will talk the subject over, if I am able to attend and what could not be written might perhaps take the form of a Resolution.

Believe me, dear Sir,
Faithfully yours
Joaquim Nabuco

Letter 11
Buxton to Nabuco

20 July 1900

Dear Sir,

I thank you for your letter of 15th inst. [letter 10] I regret that you are unable to send us a paper, but I too notice in the programme of the Congress that the subjects which are chiefly to be dealt with are rather present and future issues than past history. We have sent in four papers, treating of Egypt, Morocco and East Africa.

The Society is sending four delegates to the Congress, including the President, two members of the Committee, and myself. I think you already know Mr. Alexander, as well as Sir Fowell Buxton, and it is very good of you to propose to meet our representatives if you are able to attend.[9]

We expect to reach Paris on August 6th, and if you will be there, I hope that we may have the honour of meeting you.

I am, dear Sir
Your faithful servant
Travers Buxton

9 Nabuco did finally write a paper and presented to the congress on 7 August. See Joaquim Nabuco, *Escriptos e discursos literários* (Rio de Janeiro and Paris: Garnier, 1901), pp. 265–75.

Letter 12
Allen to Nabuco

31 July 1900
17 Well Walk, Hampstead

Dear Senhor Nabuco

I am glad to see by *The Times* that you are in London and I hope to call upon you at the Legation before long. The great heat has rather upset me.

With sincere congratulations and hoping you are quite well.

I am
Yours very truly
Chas. H. Allen

Letter 13
Allen to Nabuco

8 March 1901
17 Well Walk, Hampstead

My dear friend

I am proud to be able to call you Excellency but still prefer the older title of friend. It is many years since we first met in the interests of the Slave and I remember escorting you to the house of the Hon. Secretary Mr Joseph Cooper, then lying on his deathbed. The other Hon. Sec. Mr Sturge you knew well, for he did not die until 1893.

A shameful attack made upon him by the *Financial News* caught my eye by chance and I felt stirred to write a defence. The editor published it, and you will see it in the *Reporter*, p 19 which I now enclose, with the hearty good wishes of myself and wife.

Yours very sincerely
Chas. H. Allen

Letter 14
Buxton to Nabuco

20 June 1901

My dear Sir

Mr. Henry Gurney[10] has asked me to let you know what action has been taken by this Society in regard to slave-holding in Morocco by natives and Jews under European consular protection. In 1895 trustworthy information was received by the Society that a considerable amount of slave trading was carried on in Morocco by Jewish protégés of England and other Powers, the slaves being nominally purchased by Moors for Jewish friends – the Jews not being allowed to hold slaves.

Mr. Allen (the then Secretary) wrote to the Press to this effect in April 1895 and a few weeks later, he again wrote saying that the Legations of England, France, and Spain had taken action, but that the Consular Agents in Morocco of Brazil and the United States declined to do so, and that their protégés held more slaves than those of any other power. Accordingly in July 1896 this Committee wrote to H. E. the Brazilian Minister in London, and to the American Ambassador, bringing these facts before them and asking that the authorities representing these governments would withdraw their protection from those who abused it. Replies were received from both of these Ministers, not admitting knowledge of the abuses referred to.

Mr. Henry Gurney, on his return from Morocco last year, reported to our Committee that he believed there were about 80 persons in Mogadir under Brazilian consular protection, and he had found a case of a Brazilian protégé at Casablanca who had bought a slave. Mr. Gurney proposed that the Committee should communicate with you on this matter, but owing to our not having your correct address, the matter dropped.

I have the honour to be, Sir,
Yours truly
Travers Buxton

10 No information available on Henry Gurney and his relationship to the Anti-Slavery Society.

Letter 15
Gurney to Nabuco

21 June 1901
Reigate

Dear Sir

I hear from the Secretary of the B. and F. Anti-Slavery Society, in returning your kind letter to me of the 18th instant,[11] that my proposal to communicate with you on the subject of the holding of slaves by Brazilian protégés which was agreed to by the Committee in May last year, was after all not carried out. I apologise to you very sincerely for the mistake I made. I was talking the matter over with the Secretary before writing and should have referred back to our minutes before writing so positively.

Mr. Travers Buxton says he will write you on the subject. There is now a gentleman in England who would give you the latest information on the subject, who has taken great interest in the subject of consular protection, and who I consider to be one of the best authorities on it. I allude to Mr. Allan Maclean, British Consul at Casablanca, now attending on the Moorish envoy, whose address is 84 Lancaster Gate, W.

I have also brought the matter to the notice of Sir. Arthur Nicolson Bart, the British Minister to Morocco, whose address is Travellers' Club, Pall Mall. W., and I feel sure that either of these gentlemen would be able to satisfy you as to the necessity of some inquiry being made into the protection in Morocco by Brazilian consuls. The former gentleman is probably the best qualified as protection has been carried on to a greater extent in the south of the country.

If I could in my way assist you to get into communication with the above gentlemen I should be very pleased.

I am, dear Sir,
Yours truly,
Henry Gurney

11 Letter not found.

Letter 16
Allen to Nabuco

6 March 1902
17 Well Walk, Hampstead

My dear Excellency

You must have thought me remiss in not replying sooner to your kindly New Year greeting. But you will I know excuse me when I tell you that a serious difference in opinion with the present management of the British and Foreign Anti-Slavery Society has resulted in the resignation of myself and of my brother Joseph who has been Treasurer of the Society for nearly 23 years.[12] We regret it very much but it was inevitable.

You ask for my photograph, *which I gladly enclose*, and quite thought I had sent it you before. The weather has really been dreadful with such a long continuance of cold fog. I hope it has not upset you or Madame Nabuco. Have you been to Rome yet?[13] Your dear little parrot has borne the cold splendidly – but we take such care of him he never feels it. He is a great pet with my girls but we have to cover him up when he screams.

We all join in kindest regards and best wishes to you both and are very sorry to hear that you suffered so much from our cold climate.

Yours very sincerely
Chas. H. Allen

12 Joseph Allen was treasurer of the Society 1879–1902.

13 Nabuco went to Rome at the beginning of 1903 to present to the King of Italy his report in support of Brazil's case in the dispute with Great Britain over British Guiana.

Letter 17
Allen to Nabuco

2 April 1902
17 Well Walk, Hampstead

My dear Excellency

You will see by the enclosed[14] that my severance from the Society is now quite complete. It is a pity, though in some respects I am glad to be free from all responsibilities, and from all intercourse with the pro Boer section of our Committee.[15]

At the annual meeting next Friday they will have to explain how it is that the Society has now neither a Treasurer nor an Hon. Sec. Hoping you are both well and with hearty thanks for your very kind letter – which has been followed by very sympathetic ones from the King of the Belgians, Lord Cromer, Sir G. J. Goldie etc.

I am yours very sincerely
Chas. H. Allen

14 Enclosure not found.

15 This suggests that the Boer war (1899–1902) was the cause of the differences of opinion within the committee of the Anti-Slavery Society which led to the resignation of Charles Allen and his brother Joseph (see letter 16). The Allens belonged to the group that supported the British government; another group supported the Boers.

Letter 18
Buxton to Nabuco

9 July 1902

My dear Sir

I am directed by our Committee to ask your kind attention, as Corresponding Member of this Society, to the facts relating to the colony of Angola which are stated in the enclosed letter from a Canadian missionary who does not at present wish his name published.[16]

Within the last few months we have had brought to our notice many statements from various sources, including British Consular reports, as to the enslaving and ill treatment of the natives in Angola, and especially as to the export of 'serviçaes' from Angola to San Thomé.

Quite recently I have had personal visits from three gentlemen including the writer of this letter, who, on their return from Angola, have wished to make known to our Society the facts which have come within their own experiences.

Our Committee venture to ask you if you can advise any steps which can possibly be taken to bring these abuses, directly or indirectly, to the notice of the responsible Portuguese government, as they would appear to be in direct violation of the engagements entered into by signatories of the Brussels Act, and of the 6th and 9th Articles of the Berlin General Act of 1885.

I remain, Sir
Yours faithfully
Travers Buxton

16 Letter not found.

III Epilogue
Correspondence December 1904–January 1905

Letter 1 (draft)
Nabuco to Mrs Allen

22 December 1904
52 Cornwall Gardens

Dear Mrs. Allen

On my return after a two years absence[1] I receive the news of the great loss you are mourning[2] and I beg you to believe that in no memory, outside his intimate circle, will his features remain more vivid than in mine. He was a burning heart ['soul' deleted], I well felt the fervour of his devotion to the noble ideals that sprung for him from his powerful realization of God's presence and interest ['inspiration' deleted] in his work. I will never forget him and would be glad to contribute my part to any humble sign ['symbol' deleted] the Anti-Slavery family may wish to create in order to gather his name and keep it alive among the partisans of that undying cause.

Yours very sincerely
Joaquim Nabuco
Please kindly express to sorrow to all around you.

1 Nabuco had spent the best part of two years in Italy presenting Brazil's case in the dispute over British Guiana. On 14 June 1904 King Victor Emmanuel had found in favour of Great Britain. Nabuco was shocked by the decision. In a letter to his wife, Evelina Torres Soares Ribeiro, on 14 June he confessed: 'Listening to the King read his arbitral award, which was a victory for England, was probably the most terrible quarter of an hour I have ever endured'. And three days later: 'I did all that was possible for me to do . . . I am not going to commit suicide because we lost . . . Having fulfilled my obligations to the best of my ability, I have an easy conscience, but my heart bleeds with sorrow. I feel as if I am the mutilated one and not Brazil'. Carolina Nabuco, *Life of Joaquim Nabuco*, p. 299.

2 Charles Allen had died on 19 December 1904, aged 80.

Letter 2
Mrs Allen to Nabuco

12 January 1905
17 Well Walk, Hampstead

Dear Senhor Nabuco

It was a great pleasure to me to receive, in the midst of my trouble, your kind and sympathetic letter [letter 1], and I thank you much for it.

My dear husband had a long and painful illness, beginning with an attack of bronchitis (which the doctors consider must have been influenza) two years ago. This was followed by severe neuritis in the right arm and shoulder, causing intense pain, and ever since he has suffered from this complaint, one attack succeeding another in spite of all that medical science and the best advice in London could do. In time both arms were affected and became powerless, so that he was dependent on others for everything, but he had the devoted attention of the whole household, who were only too delighted to wait on him. We had also a very nice trained nurse who was a great comfort to us. It was truly sad to see him suffer so much at times, though he was wonderfully patient; but as his general health kept very good we hoped that the neuritis might eventually be overcome, and so for some time did his doctors – but it was not be.

He took great interest in public affairs and had *The Times* read to him every day. Until quite lately, he did not look like an invalid, and I wish you could have paid him a visit as many of his friends did, but you were away, I believe, the whole time that he was ill. I know what a great regard, I may say affection you had for each other, and I know too how much you appreciated his fine character, and the excellent work he did for the oppressed. I shall always have a pleasant memory of the visit he and I paid to you and Mme Nabuco in Cornwall Gardens and also of the interesting function at Westminster Abbey for which you gave us tickets of admission.

To turn from sad things to bright ones, I and my children heartily congratulate you on your new and important appointment, which is announced in this morning's paper.[3] I am sure you will fill the office most worthily and to the benefit of both countries. The only drawback seems to me the climate, which in winter I'm afraid Mme Nabuco may find rather too severe. With kindest regards to you both, believe me

3 Nabuco had been invited by barão do Rio Branco, the minister of foreign relations, to become Brazilian ambassador to the United States.

Yours very sincerely
Sarah E. Allen

The parrot you presented to us is in beautiful condition and is a great pet, especially with my daughter Beatrice who takes him out of his cage on to her hand. He was quite tame with Charles and her but with no one else. When he heard dear Charles' voice, if we placed him at the foot of the stairs he would climb up them to the bedroom. He would then climb up on to his knee and remain there quite quietly.

I hope your family are well.

Letter 3
Nabuco to Mrs Allen

13 January 1905
London

Dear Mrs. Allen

Many thanks for your so kind letter [letter 2]. I see in it the fortitude with which you bear your great misfortune, and that more than anything tells the comfort that truly Religion is. It is so much like himself the picture you make of his patience in illness and forced quiet. With his active mind and frame! Yes I greatly appreciated him and wish some record of the love of so many could survive us, although now he has already attained a much greater reward in Infinite Love.

The other day I read a story of a parrot of Mme. Patti that explains the case of your old dumb parrot. One was given to her as a fine speaking bird, but never spoke, except much later, when the Doctor entering to see her he startled both (probably he felt also ill then) by mimicking her. 'Doctor, I feel so sick'. Perhaps yours will some day throw off the mask of silence, but choosing, I trust, a brighter occasion.[4]

Many thanks for your congratulation (of all of you) on my appointment. We leave England with regret, but will join our new post with delight, as every charge in public life must be pleasurably taken in order to be well accomplished.[5]

With our kindest regards to you and your children
Yours very truly
J.N.

---

4 Nabuco was mistaken here. It was the first of the two parrots he gave the Allens that was dumb.

5 Nabuco left for Washington in May 1905. He died there on 17 January 1910.

Chronology

1783
Committee on the Slave Traffic formed in London by the Quakers

1787
Committee for the Abolition of the Slave Trade formed in London

1807
Abolition of the slave trade by the British Parliament

1810
Anglo-Portuguese Treaty under which Portugal commits itself to abolish the slave trade gradually and in the meantime to limit it to its own colonies

1815
Anglo-Portuguese Treaty under which Portugal abolishes the slave trade north of the Equator

1823
Society for the Mitigation and Gradual Abolition of Slavery throughout the British Dominions (the Anti-Slavery Society) formed in London

1826
Anglo-Brazilian Treaty under which Brazil was obliged to abolish the slave trade three years after ratification of the treaty (in March 1827)

1831
9 November: Law declaring the importation of slaves into Brazil illegal

1833
Abolition of slavery throughout the British Empire (from 1 August 1834)

1839
April: Formation of the British and Foreign Anti-Slavery Society
June: Formation of the Society for the Extinction of the Slave Trade and the Civilization of Africa (closed in 1843)

1840
January: First issue of the *Anti-Slavery Reporter*, the journal of the British and Foreign Anti Slavery Society

June: First World Anti-Slavery Convention in London

1850
4 September: Brazilian law for suppression of the illegal slave trade – effectively enforced 1850-1

1865
January: 13th amendment to the Constitution abolishing slavery in the United States

1866
January: Pimenta Bueno, at the request of the Emperor Dom Pedro II, presents five Abolitionist projects
July: French Emancipation Committee appeal to the Emperor in favour of abolition
August: Emperor's reply

1867
April: First reference to emancipation in a Speech from the Throne
August: International Slavery Conference in Paris

1869
August: Message to the Brazilian people from the International Abolitionist Association in Paris in favour of abolition
Setember: Conde d'Eu abolishes slavery in Paraguay at the end of the Paraguayan War

1870
Nabuco writes a student text *A escravidão*, not published in his lifetime
November: Nabuco graduates from the Law Faculty in Recife

1871
28 September: Law of Free Birth

1873
31 August: Nabuco embarks on his first visit to Europe

1874
June: Nabuco in London
25 September: Nabuco returns to Brazil

1876
7 June: Nabuco leaves for the United States via Europe to take up the post of attaché at the Brazilian legation in Washington
August: Senator Nabuco de Araújo promotes the candidature of his son for deputy in Pernambuco

1877
21 October: Nabuco arrives in London as attaché at the Brazilian legation

1878
5 January: Liberal Party under the Visconde de Sinimbu takes power for the first time in 10 years
19 March: Death in Rio de Janeiro of senator Nabuco de Araújo
30 April: Nabuco arrives back in Brazil
5 September: Joaquim Nabuco (aged 29) elected to the Chamber of Deputies for Recife

1879
10 January: Nabuco takes his seat in the Chamber

1880
8 January: first known contact between Nabuco and the British and Foreign Anti-Slavery Society
30 January: Spanish Congress abolishes slavery in Cuba, but with eight years' *patronato*
26 August: bill to end slavery by 1890 presented to the Chamber by Nabuco, fails to find support and is withdrawn
7 September: Sociedade Brasileira contra a Escravidão founded by Nabuco and others in Rio de Janeiro
1 November: first issue of *O Abolicionista*, journal of the Sociedade Brasileira contra Escravidao
December: Nabuco embarks again for Europe

1881
January: Nabuco received by the Câmara dos Deputados in Lisboa and the Sociedade Abolicionista Espanhola in Madrid
February-April: Nabuco in London
10 May: Nabuco arrives back in Rio de Janeiro
30 June: Chamber of Deputies dissolved
3 October: Nabuco defeated in elections for Rio de Janeiro
1 December: last number of *O Abolicionista*
December: Nabuco leaves for London (and stays until April 1884)

1883
May: Confederacao Abolicionista formed in Rio de Janeiro
August: publication of Nabuco's *O Abolicionismo* in London

1884
25 March: abolition of slavery in Ceara
17 May: Nabuco returns to Rio de Janeiro
6 June: Dantas cabinet introduces bill to free slaves at 60
10 July: abolition of slavery in Amazonas
28 July: Chamber supports by 59 votes to 52 motion of no confidence in Dantas cabinet
3 September: Chamber dissolved. Nabuco candidate for first district of Pernambuco (Recife)
1 December: election in Recife annulled

1885
9 January: Nabuco elected in Recife
4 May: Dantas defeated in new vote of confidence by 52 votes to 50 and resigns
6 May: Saraiva replaces Dantas as president of the Council of Ministers. Dantas bill modified, introducing indemnification clause
12 May: Chamber fails to recognise Nabuco's election in Recife
7 June: Nabuco elected to Chamber for fifth district of Pernambuco
13 August: Saraiva bill approved by Chamber. Saraiva then resigns
20 August: Emperor invites Conservative leader Barao de Cotegipe to form a government. Cotegipe promises to secure Senate approval for Saraiva bill
24 August: Chamber passes motion of no confidence in Cotegipe cabinet by 63 votes to 49
28 September: Law of Sexagenarians (Saraiva-Cotegipe Law)
26 October: Chamber dissolved by Cotegipe

1886
15 January: Nabuco defeated in elections for Chamber in Recife
October: abolition of *patronato* in Cuba

1887
April-August: Nabuco in London
30 June: Emperor to Europe for health reasons; Princess Isabel assumes Regency
26 August: Nabuco returns to Recife to contest by-election

14 September: Nabuco elected to Chamber in Recife
5 October: Nabuco assumes seat in Chamber
29 November: Nabuco leaves for Europe
15 December: Nabuco arrives in London

1888
11 Janeiro: Nabuco arrives in Rome
10 February: Audience with Pope Leão XIII
March-April: Nabuco in London
10 March: Cotegipe resigns. Princess Isabel invites another Conservative João Alfredo to form a government committed to abolition of slavery
30 March: Nabuco arrives in Recife from Europe
18 April: Nabuco in Rio de Janeiro
3 May: opening of Parliament
8 May: bill for immediate abolition without indemnification presented to the Chamber
9 May: bill approved on second reading 83 votes to nine
10 May: third reading in Chamber and bill sent to Senate
11 May: bill presented to Senate
12 May: bill approved on second reading, six votes against
13 May: bill approved on third reading in Senate
15:00 hours: the Princess Regent in the Paço da Cidade signs the Lei Áurea abolishing slavery in Brazil

Bibliography

Primary sources

(i) Manuscript:

Nabuco correspondence in:
Rhodes House, Oxford
Fundação Joaquim Nabuco, Recife
Arquivo do Itamaraty, Rio de Janeiro
Instituto Histórico e Geográfico Brasileiro (coleção Wanderley Pinho), Rio de Janeiro

(ii) Printed:

Annaes do Parlamento Brazileiro. Câmara dos Deputados
Coleção de Leis do Império do Brasil
Gazeta de Notícias
Jornal do Commercio
Manifesto da Sociedade Brasileira contra a Escravidão [1880].
Organizações e programas ministeriais. Regime parlamentar no Império [1889] (Rio de Janeiro: Arquivo Nacional, 1962)
O Abolicionista
Malheiro, Agostinho Marques Perdigão. *A escravidão no Brasil: ensaio histórico-jurídico-socia*l [1866]. 3rd. ed.: Petrópolis: Vozes, 1976
Rebouças, André. *Diário e notas autobiográficas*. Rio de Janeiro: José Olympio, 1938
The *Anti-Slavery Reporter*
The *Rio News*
The Times

(iii) Writings of Joaquim Nabuco:

A escravidão [1870]. *Revista do Instituto Histórico e Geográfico Brasileiro* vol. 204, 1949. 2nd. ed. Recife and Brasília: Editora Massangana and CNPq, 1988.

Campanha abolicionista no Recife (eleições de 1884). Preface by Aníbal Falcão. Rio de Janeiro, 1885. 2nd facsimile edition Recife: Fundacao Joaquim Nabuco/Editora Massangana, 1988. 3rd ed. Brasília: Senado Federal/ Fundação Casa Rui Barbosa, introduction by Manoel Correia de Andrade, 1992.

Campanhas de imprensa, 1884–1887. São Paulo: Instituto Progresso Editorial, 1949. *Obras completas*, vol. XII

Cartas a amigos. Edited by Carolina Nabuco. Vol. 1, 1864-98. São Paulo: Instituto Progresso Editorial S.A., 1949. *Obras completas* vols. XIII e XIV

Cartas aos abolicionistas ingleses. Edited by José Thomaz Nabuco. Recife: Fundação Joaquim Nabuco/Editora Massangana, 1985.

Diários vol. 1 1873-88, vol.2 1889–1910. Preface and notes by Evaldo Cabral de Mello. Rio de Janeiro: Editora Bem-Te-Vi and Recife: Editora Massangana, 2005.

Congresso Agrícola de 1878. Facsimile edition. Introduction by José Murilo de Carvalho. Rio de Janeiro: Fundação Casa de Rui Barbosa, 1988.

Discursos parlamentares, 1879–1889. São Paulo: Instituto Progresso Editorial, 1949. *Obras completas* vol. XI

Eleições liberais e eleições conservadoras. Rio de Janeiro: Leuzinger, 1886.

Escriptos e discursos literários. Rio de Janeiro and Paris: Garnier, 1901.

Minha Formação. Rio de Janeiro: Garnier, 1900; Senado Federal, Brasília 1998; Rio de Janeiro, Topbooks, 1999.

O Abolicionismo. London: Abraham Kingdon, 1883; Rio de Janeiro, Nova Fronteira, 1999. Eng. trans. by Robert Conrad: *Abolitionism. The Brazilian anti-slavery struggle*, Urbana, Illinois: University of Illinois Press, 1977.

O eclypse do abolicionismo. Rio de Janeiro: Leuzinger, 1886.

O erro do imperador. Rio de Janeiro: Leuzinger, 1886.

Um estadista do Império: Nabuco de Araújo, sua vida, suas opiniões, sua época. Rio de Janeiro: Garnier, 1897–1898. 3 vols. 4th ed.: Rio de Janeiro: Nova Aguilar, 1975.

Secondary sources

Alonso, Angela (2007) *Joaquim Nabuco*. São Paulo: Companhia das Letras.

Bethell, Leslie (1970) *The abolition of the Brazilian slave trade. Britain, Brazil and the slave trade question 1807–1869*, Cambridge: Cambridge University Press. Port. trans.: *A abolição do tráfico de escravos no Brasil*, Rio de Janeiro: Editôra Expressão e Cultura/Editôra Universidade de São Paulo (1976); *A abolição do comércio brasileiro de escravos*, Brasília: Editora do Senado Federal (2002).

Bethell, Leslie (ed.) (1989) *Brazil: Empire and Republic, 1822–1930.* Cambridge: Cambridge University Press.

Bethell, Leslie (1991) 'The decline and fall of slavery in nineteenth century Brazil', *Transactions of the Royal Historical Society*, 6th series, vol. 1.

Carvalho, José Murilo de (2006) *A construção da ordem: a elite política imperial* e *Teatro de Sombras: a política imperial.* Rio de Janeiro: Civilização Brasileira.

Carvalho, Jose Murilo de (2007) *D. Pedro II: ser ou não ser*. São Paulo: Companhia das Letras.

Conrad, Robert (1972) *The destruction of Brazilian slavery, 1850-1888.* Berkeley: University of California Press. Port. trans.: *Os últimos anos da escravatura no Brasil: 1850-1888.* Rio de Janeiro: Civilização Brasileira (1975).

Davies, David Brion (2006) *Inhuman bondage. The rise and fall of slavery in the New World.* New York: Oxford University Press.

Eakin, Marshall C. (1989) *British enterprise in Brazil. The St. John d'el Rey Mining Company and the Morro Velho gold mine, 1830-1960.* Durham N.C.: Duke University Press.

Mendonça, Joseli Maria Nunes (1999) *Entre a mão e os anéis: a lei dos sexagenários e os caminhos da abolição no Brasil.* Campinas: Editora Unicamp.

Mendonça, Renato de (1942) *Um diplomata na corte da Inglaterra* [Penedo]. Rio de Janeiro: Companhia Editora Nacional.

Moraes, Evaristo de (1924) *A campanha abolicionista, 1879–1888.* Rio de Janeiro. 2nd ed.: Brasília: Editora da Universidade de Brasília (1986).

Nabuco, Carolina (1928) *Vida de Joaquim Nabuco, por sua filha.* São Paulo: Companhia Editora Nacional. Eng. trans. by Ronald Hilton : *The life of Joaquim Nabuco.* Stanford: Stanford University Press (1950).

Salles, Ricardo (2002) *Joaquim Nabuco. Um pensador do Império.* Rio de Janeiro: Topbooks.

Sandroni, Cícero (2007) *180 anos do Jornal do Commercio, 1827–2007.* Rio de Janeiro: Quorum Editora Ltda.

Silva, Leonardo Dantas (1988) *A imprensa e a abolição.* Recife: Fundação Joaquim Nabuco/Editora Massangana.

Viana Filho, Luiz (1973) *A vida de Joaquim Nabuco.* São Paulo: Martins.

INSTITUTE FOR THE STUDY OF THE
AMERICAS
UNIVERSITY OF LONDON · SCHOOL OF ADVANCED STUDY

The Institute for the Study of the Americas (ISA) promotes, coordinates and provides a focus for research and postgraduate teaching on the Americas – Canada, the USA, Latin America and the Caribbean – in the University of London.

The Institute was officially established in August 2004 as a result of a merger between the Institute of Latin American Studies and the Institute of United States Studies, both of which were formed in 1965.

The Institute publishes in the disciplines of history, politics, economics, sociology, anthropology, geography and environment, development, culture and literature, and on the countries and regions of Latin America, the United States, Canada and the Caribbean.

ISA runs an active programme of events – conferences, seminars, lectures and workshops – in order to facilitate national research on the Americas in the humanities and social sciences. It also offers a range of taught master's and research degrees, allowing wide-ranging multi-disciplinary, multi-country study or a focus on disciplines such as politics or globalisation and development for specific countries or regions.

Full details about the Institute's publications, events, postgraduate courses and other activities are available on the web at www.americas.sas.ac.uk.

Institute for the Study of the Americas
School of Advanced Study, University of London
Senate House, Malet Street, London WC1E 7HU

Tel 020 7862 8870, Fax 020 7862 8886, Email americas@sas.ac.uk
Web www.americas.sas.ac.uk

Recent and forthcoming titles in the ISA series:

Democracy after Pinochet: Politics, parties and elections in Chile (2007)
by Alan Angell

Mexican Soundings: Essays in Honour of David A. Brading (2007)
edited by Susan Deans-Smith and Eric Van Young

America's Americans: Population Issues in U.S. Society and Politics (2007)
edited by Philip Davies and Iwan Morgan

Football in the Americas: Fútbol, Futebol, Soccer (2007)
edited by Rory Miller

Bolivia: Revolution and the Power of History in the Present. Essays (2007)
James Dunkerley

American Civilization (2007)
Charles A. Jones

Caribbean Literature After Independence: The Case of Earl Lovelace (2008)
edited by Bill Schwarz

The Political Economy of the Public Budget in the Americas (2008)
edited by Diego Sánchez-Ancochea and Iwan Morgan

Contesting Clio's Craft: New Directions and Debates in Canadian History (forthcoming)
edited by Christopher Dummitt & Michael Dawson

The Contemporary Canadian Metropolis (forthcoming)
edited by Richard Dennis, Ceri Morgan and Stephen Shaw

Latin London: The Lives of Latin American Migrants in the Capital (forthcoming)
by Cathy McIlwaine

Printed in the United States
213082BV00002B/3/P